NEW HAVEN AND NORTHAMPTON CANAL GREENWAY

NEW HAVEN AND NORTHAMPTON CANAL GREENWAY

BY: ROBERT R. MADISON

Silver Street Media

NEW HAVEN AND NORTHAMPTON CANAL GREENWAY
BIKE AND RAIL TRAILS

Cover art: Robert R. Madison
Book layout: Danielle Weaver

ISBN 978-0-9979508-0-9 (paperback)
ISBN 978-0-9979508-1-6 (hardcover)

Silver Street Media

Proudly printed and bound in the U.S.A. by
Bridgeport National Bindery, Inc., Agawam, Massachusetts

HISTORIC CANAL SIGNAGE

Thank you for buying this book. All author's income from this book goes directly to the Southwick Historic Society, Inc. specifically to purchase the above historic roadside signage. You can also send a donation directly to the Southwick Historic Society, Inc. As the fund grows each of the sixteen community historic societies along the rail trail will continue to receive similar signage for their highways and byways (with their own historical society name on the bottom of the sign). Just write on the check: for canal signage.

The canal passed through sixteen communities when it was in operation. Today, many do not realize the New Haven & Northampton Canal actually existed and was in operation from 1828 to 1847. The purpose of this fund is to place New Haven & Northampton Canal Crossing signage along highways and byways as the canal linked New Haven and Northampton, a canal distance of some 87 miles.

Why? It's historic. And, progress is slowly destroying the canal. Maybe these historic roadside signs will alert everyone that something historic once occurred in this space.

Southwick Historic Society, Inc., P.O. Box 323, Southwick, MA 01077
www.southwickhistoricalsociety.org

NEW HAVEN AND NORTHAMPTON CANAL GREENWAY

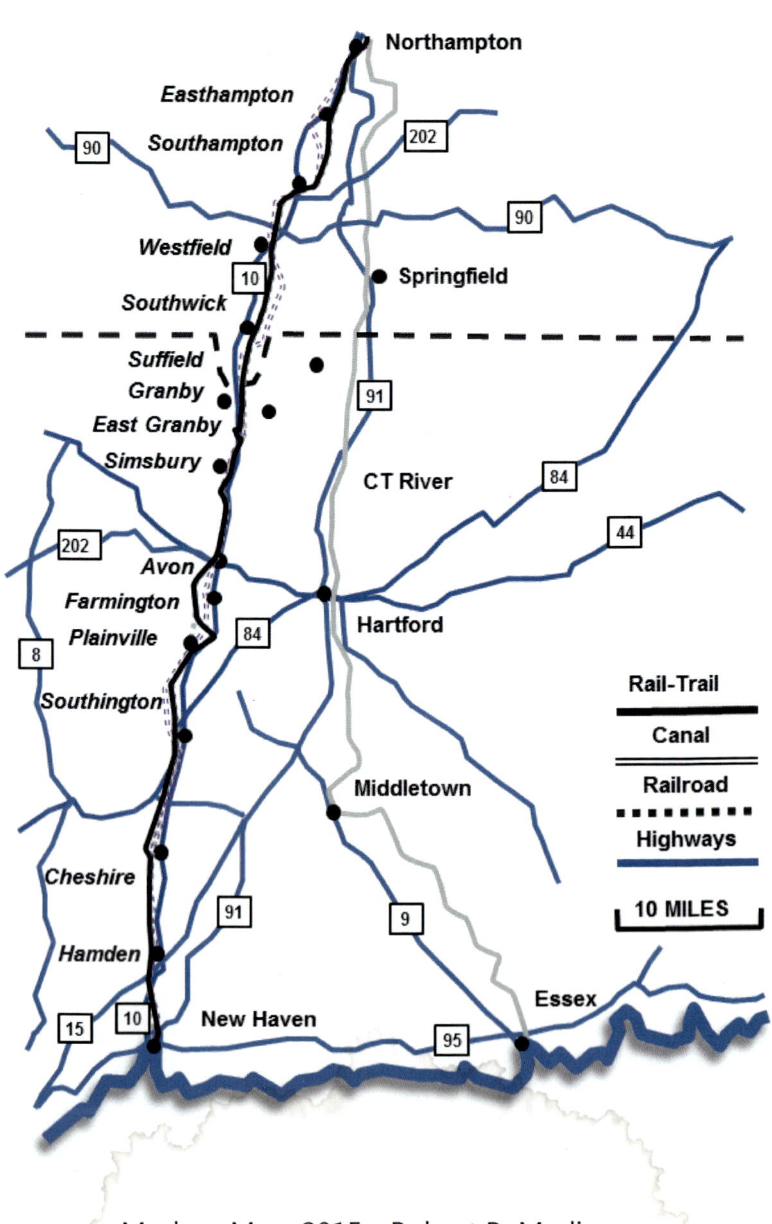

Modern Map, 2015 - Robert R. Madison

CONTENTS

NEW HAVEN AND NORTHAMPTON CANAL GREENWAY

FOREWORD BY CRAIG DELLA PENNA

Craig Della Penna is widely recognized as the foremost expert on rail trails in the Northeast. He worked for twenty years in the railroad industry and for eight years as the New England Field Representative for the Rails to Trails Conservancy. Craig is the author of rail trail guides to New England, New York, and New Jersey. Based in Northampton, Massachusetts, he operates a rail trail consulting firm, Northeast Greenway Solutions, and has a real estate practice specializing in homes near rail trails or other conservation lands. He can be reached by email at craig@greenwaysolutions.org.

In 2016 we'll be celebrating the 50th anniversary of the National Historic Preservation Act which was passed by Congress in 1966. An interesting convergence of events both bad and good came about in the early 1960s. With Jacqueline Kennedy's high profile TV tour of the White House and the renovations there during her husband's short tenure, she introduced the concept of historic preservation to the citizens of the U.S.

One of her lesser-known historic preservation efforts succeeded in created a better outcome for a development in DC's Lafayette Square near the White House where the early plan called for demolishing a neighborhood of historic structures. In the late 1960s she was instrumental in making sure that Grand Central Terminal in New York City was not demolished.

These early efforts in advocacy for historic preservation led to the energizing of the National Trust for Historic Preservation as a leader in the advocacy for other nationally significant and iconic places or buildings. In 1963, in the Chicago Tribune, a letter to the editor by May Watts calling for the saving of a former RR corridor for a walking/bike pathway is generally seen as the catalyst that launched the rail-to-trail efforts [linear parks] across the U.S.

One of the earlier rail-to-trail type projects in Connecticut was actually originally built as a canal in the 1800's. It was not a commercial success and the right-of-way of the canal later became a railroad. By the late 1980s, after sections of the railroad were being abandoned, advocacy efforts began to call for an effort, looking to convert the use of the corridor, one more time. This time as a bike and hike trail. The first sections to be converted were in CT—outside of New Haven in Cheshire. Efforts--originally led by Nancy Alderman of Hamden, CT took years to gain traction, but today much of the R-o-W in CT has been converted and Massachusetts too has much of the corridor already converted to a trail or is at least in the planning stages. At over 80 miles, it is the longest interstate trail in New England.

These linear parks are historic preservation projects in their own right. Reclaiming and rebuilding what has been lost or forgotten to become useful for public recreation, transportation and enjoyment. What is very exciting about this book is that it is the first one that specifically focuses on this corridor, showing exactly where all the lost pieces are, but telling in a nicely written story, not only what happened along the way, but things you find along the way. Bob Madison is also to be commended for his making the proceeds of this effort available to communities along the corridor for the installation of signage that'll call out information about this forgotten place. Historic preservation takes many forms.

NEW HAVEN AND NORTHAMPTON CANAL GREENWAY

FOREWORD BY CARL E. WALTER

Historian and retired physician, Dr. Carl E. Walter has been studying the New Haven and Northampton Canal since 1991. Mr. Walter has created the only maps of the canal as it meandered through the canal towns of Connecticut and Massachusetts. He has walked the canal twice and consulted with libraries and historical societies along the canal towns. He is a noted lecturer and advocate of keeping the canal history alive by giving tours and visiting local historical societies.

THE CANAL AND ITS IMPACT ON THE CANAL GREENWAY

BY DR. CARL E. WALTER

Bob Madison has written a comprehensive guide to the linear park that connects New Haven, Connecticut with Northampton, Massachusetts. His book describes the current iteration of the two separate transportation rights of way that preceded the creation of the park. These rights of way once belonged to the New Haven and Northampton Company, one for use as a canal and the other for use as a railroad. In Connecticut, between New Haven and northern Cheshire, both rights of way are almost identical, but as they proceed north they diverge and only occasionally intersect at places where the topography is favorable to both. This is the case because, while both the canal and the railroad are seeking the shortest route between New Haven and Northampton, the engineering and construction of each vary considerably.

The canal was 'paved' with water and provided a smooth, low-friction surface along which heavy loads could be pulled far more easily than by using draft animals to pull wagons over primitive roads. However, canal water must be kept level both to contain it within the canal and to prevent a flow of water that would impede navigation. As the canal climbed rapidly from Long Island Sound to Cheshire the level of the canal needed to be changed frequently. This was accomplished in steps using locks which followed a direct route from one level to another as the canal moved inland. These locks were necessary parts of the canal, but were expensive to build, maintain, and operate. For these reasons their uses need to be kept to a minimum.

Once the canal had climbed from sea level to the 'Cheshire Summit', the elevation of the land to the north increased more gradually. Here the canal's engineers sought a route that minimized the use of locks by keeping the levels of the canal constant for the longest possible distances. North of the Cheshire swamps this was accomplished by siting the canal at the required elevations along the existing contours of the land. Further inland, as the land continued to rise, these elevations became increasingly more difficult to locate, and to avoid the construction of additional locks, the canal was forced to follow a progressively more sinuous route.

A railroad, on the other hand, is 'paved' with solid metal rails anchored to the ground. The friction between these rails and a locomotive's wheels allows for constant gradual changes in elevation along a more direct route than is possible with a canal's strictly level right of way. This is the reason why the canal and railroad rights of way diverged north of the /Cheshire summit and share common ground to the north only when the topography is mutually beneficial. North of Cheshire the linear park more closely follows the railroad right of way.

By 1840 it became apparent that railroads cost less than canals to build, maintain, and operate. In addition, railroads were less vulnerable to acts of nature, offered faster more direct transportation, and could operate year around. In 1846, with two decades of the canal's financial difficulties behind it and the promise of a railroad before it, the New

Haven & Northampton Company applied to have its charter changed from that of a canal to that of a railroad. By the time the canal was abandoned in 1848 rails had been laid between New Haven and Plainville. In 1856, after several delays, the company's railroad reached Northampton thus replacing the canal with more up to date mode of transportation located on a substantially different right of way.

Those curious about the canal's history might be interested in the appended synopsis.

Between 1835 and 1847 a canal connected New Haven, Connecticut and Northampton, Massachusetts, much as Interstate Highway 91 does today. In Connecticut the Farmington Canal ran 56 miles from New Haven Harbor on Long Island Sound to the state's northern border in West Suffield. Here it joined the Hampshire and Hampden Canal which extended 31 miles from Massachusetts southern border in Southwick to the Connecticut River in Northampton. Both canals were built to the same specifications and were consolidated as the New Haven and Northampton Canal in 1836.

In the early Nineteenth Century overland transportation in New England was very difficult. Travel in coaches and wagons was physically demanding, time consuming, and expensive. Many roads were little more than dirt trails widened just enough to allow the passage of wagons. Even the best roads were unpaved, ungraded, rocky, and rutted with steep inclines up and down hillsides. The scarcity of bridges and culverts made crossing rivers and streams difficult and time consuming. Land transportation was so difficult that it cost a New Haven merchant as much to transport a ton of goods thirty-three miles to Farmington, Connecticut as it did to make the same shipment by sea to London, England. Products manufactured more than five miles from the sea or a major river were often priced out of the market by the expense of transportation. Most people did not travel much and most products were made and consumed locally.

In the early 1800's New Haven and Hartford rivaled one another as the co-capitals of Connecticut. New Haven's location on Long Island Sound allowed its merchants fleet ready access to markets up and down the eastern seaboard of the United States and beyond. However, the expense of overland shipping limited its access to the markets of New England's interior. Hartford's inland location at the head of sloop navigation on the Connecticut River allowed contact with both Long Island Sound and New England's back country. During the early decades of the Nineteenth Century ongoing competition between the two cities induced New Haven to seek better commercial ties with the interior. The solution seemed to be a canal.

The idea of a canal stretching inland from New Haven to the Farmington River valley seems to date from the 1780's but it lay dormant for a generation as the country recovered from the Revolution and the War of 1812. About 1820 the concept was revived and expanded to include transit of the western part of Massachusetts' Pioneer Valley so as to connect New Haven harbor with the Connecticut River at Northampton.

Before the development of railroads canals were viewed as one of the best ways to improve overland transportation in the United States. Movement on the level fluid surface of a canal was easier, smoother, faster, and less expensive than travel on contemporary roads. Canal transportation compared favorably with river navigation in that there were no currents, rocks, rapids, or waterfalls to impede travel. If New Haven could construct such a passage inland it would increase the trade and commerce of the city. If New Haven could construct a canal to connect the Connecticut River upstream from Hartford much of this increase might come at Hartford's expense.

The feasibility of the project was demonstrated by a preliminary survey performed by Henry Wright and Andrew A. Bartow in 1822. Later the same year the Farmington Canal Company was granted a charter by the State of Connecticut that allowed the use of whatever land and water sources that were needed to build and operate a canal. A private stock company was organized in 1823 by a group of prominent men from towns located along the projected line of the canal. After a more detailed survey the cost of the project was estimated at $330,000. Books were opened for subscription to the company's stock on July 15, 1823.

Contracts were let for excavating the various sections of the canal, and construction of the Farmington Canal began on July 4, 1825. Experienced contractors secured contracts for some of the more specialized construction while local men and Irish immigrants dug much of the canal bed. Since the canal was built before the advent of powered construction equipment all the work was accomplished by the labor of animals and men.

Trees and stumps along the line of the canal were removed with axes, picks, shovels, and ox-powered stump pullers. The sandy soil was loosened with plows drawn by teams of oxen. Earth was moved and graded with horse carts drawn by animals. Lifting was accomplished with ropes, pulleys, and simple cranes.

The prism of the Farmington Canal was twenty feet wide at the bottom and six feet deep. The sides of the canal sloped one part upward for each two parts outward to give an operating width of thirty-six feet when the water was at the normal depth of four feet. The width the prism at the top of the canal was forty-six feet. One side of the canal (generally the downhill side) was defined by a ten foot wide tow path. The opposite side was bounded by an earth bank at least seven feet wide or perhaps a hillside.

The construction altered the landscape and disrupted the lives of those in its path as land was excavated or perhaps buried under mounds of earth. Hillsides were opened and valleys filled. Stream courses were altered and water rights affected. Roads were relocated, buildings removed, and some landowners found their property divided. In 1829 a group of three Canal Commissioners toured the line of the completed canal, heard the petitions of affected landowners and, in many cases, awarded what they felt was fair compensation for damages. Sometimes the damage was not evident until the canal was in operation and changes in the adjacent water table decreased land values. The landowners' inevitable dissatisfaction lead to legal actions against the canal company, vandalism of its works, ultimately additional expense.

By 1829 the canal was open for business between New Haven and Westfield, Massachusetts, and construction on large parts of the remainder was well advanced. However, the effort exhausted the limited financial resources of the prime contractors in Massachusetts, and in 1830 they abandoned their contracts.

From New Haven's point of view, the success of the Hampshire and Hampden Canal which would connect the Farmington Canal with the Connecticut River, was very important. In 1830 former U.S. Senator James Hillhouse, President of the Farmington Canal Company led an attempt to obtain Federal funding to complete the Hampshire and Hampden Canal. This effort failed when it was opposed by interests promoting improvement of transportation on the Connecticut River. Relief finally came in 1831 when the Connecticut Legislature chartered the City Bank of New Haven which purchased $100,000 of the capital stock of the Hampshire and Hampden Canal Company. Construction resumed in 1832, but suffered a setback in October of 1833 when the feeder dam on the Westfield River was washed away. By July of 1834 the dam was replaced and the canal was completed to Northampton. Unfortunately a water shortage resulting from poor location of the Westfield River feeder dam and the porosity of the sandy canal bed delayed the opening of the canal to Northampton until July 1835. Shortly thereafter both the Farmington Canal Company and the Hampshire and Hampden Canal Company were forced to declare bankruptcy. In 1836 the original stockholders lost their entire investment when the companies were reorganized as the New Haven and Northampton Canal Company. The original companies' remaining debts were paid with the stock of the new company.

After its first full season of operation between New Haven and Northampton the new company suffered a severe setback when a winter storm destroyed the feeder dam on the Westfield River. In 1837 the canal north of Westfield was closed almost the entire season for lack of water while the dam was relocated and rebuilt. Between 1838 and 1847 the New Haven and Northampton Canal Company operated with varying degrees of success. Lack of funds for repairs seriously delayed the opening of the seasons of 1839 and 1840. However, 1840 brought contact with shipping interests in Boston and Albany when the Western Railroad intersected the canal in Westfield. The following two seasons saw the development of substantial trade on the canal between New York City and northern New England. The season of 1843 was interrupted in October by a series of storm related washouts that required a month to repair. The following year the canal's operating season was uninterrupted, but a three month drought and serious vandalism on the Great Fill in Cheshire, Connecticut stunted the season of 1845.

During the two decades that the canal was in operation it gradually became apparent that railroads cost less to build, operate, and maintain. Furthermore rail transportation was faster, used more direct routes, and operated year around. In 1846 the New Haven and Northampton Canal Company was rechartered as a railroad and began laying rails on the tow path in southern Connecticut. The canal remained in operation during the seasons of 1846 and 1847 and was then abandoned.

NEW HAVEN AND NORTHAMPTON CANAL GREENWAY

FOREWORD BY ROBERT JOSEPH BELLETZKIE

Robert Joseph Belletzkie is a retired academic reference librarian. His TylerCityStation website shares much of what he has learned over 50 years of research. He has visited numerous repositories, given talks all over Connecticut and is currently assisting several historical societies with organizing their railroad collections. From 2008 to 2011, he processed the Board of Railroad Commissioners papers for the Connecticut State Library Archives, opening packets of documents that had been sealed for over 150 years, organizing and making them available to researchers for the first time. He lives in Prospect, CT and is a member of several historical and railroad societies. Email: rrtrax2@yahoo.com

---

The New Haven & Northampton RR has a unique history that continues to fascinate those who research it today. Begun as a canal, converted to a railroad immediately set upon by adversaries, later becoming a viable trunk line, and finally falling into the hands of its nemesis, this may sound like the stuff of legend, but these are the facts!

Modeled on New York's Erie Canal, the boats started running here in 1828, bringing considerable economic and social change to the Farmington Valley and creating an industrial corridor evident even to this day. While there were a few good years, the finances floundered. One reason was that tolls were the major source of revenue and never came close to paying the bills. Thus waterway yielded to iron rail in

1848. Held in check by rival Hartford & New York lines, the NH&N's northward progress was halting but Northampton was reached in 1856. Independent again as of 1 July 1869, the road lost no time in purchasing new equipment, modernizing facilities, and constructing Canal Dock in New Haven for water connections to New York City. On the north end, Shelburne Falls, MA was reached in 1881 with access to Albany and the West via the Troy & Greenfield's Hoosac Tunnel. Steady traffic -- freight, passenger, express, mail and milk – hustled up and down the 100-mile main line, fed by several important branches to New Hartford, CT, Holyoke, Williamsburg and Turners Falls, MA.

The Connecticut Board of Railroad Commissioners annual report for 1886 shows the NH&N with 540 employees and net earnings of $259,334.86 (about $6 million today), having logged 9,635,128 passenger-miles and 29,064,137 freight-ton miles. Respected as a competitor and seen as a target for takeover by rivals, the Canal line was leased once again in 1887 by the now all-powerful New York, New Haven & Hartford RR; the NH&N's corporate existence was extinguished in 1910. The "New Haven" came to its own end on 31 December 1968 but even in later days locals speak of 100-car trains using the line. Segments have been abandoned through subsequent bankruptcies and successive owners until Pioneer Valley in Westfield, MA and Pan Am Southern in Plainville, CT operate the only remaining portions today.

The conversion of the NH&N to rail trail, with the appropriate signage that this publication will provide, permanently extends the service life of this unique transportation corridor. Now with pedestrians, bicycles and baby carriages taking the place of mules, canal boats and rail cars, future generations will enjoy and learn about the evolution enshrined in this great linear park. 168 years and counting!

PREFACE

NEW HAVEN AND NORTHAMPTON CANAL GREENWAY

On the east coast, the longest bike route is the East Coast Greenway, some 3,000 miles of bike trails from Florida to Maine and Canada. The East Coast Greenway is made up of many, many individual bike routes. The New Haven & Northampton Canal Greenway is also made up of many individual bike trails, on street biking and rail-trails linked together by the sixteen communities the canal, railroad and now bike trails travels through.

These trails include:

- The New Haven Vision Trail
- The Farmington Canal Heritage Trail
- The Farmington Canal Trail
- Southington Rails-to-Trails
- Plainville Bicycle Travelway
- Farmington River Canal Trail
- Farmington Valley Greenway
- The Hampden & Hampshire Rail Trail
- Southwick Rail Trail
- The Westfield Colombia Greenway RailTrail
- Southampton Greenway
- New Haven – Northampton Railroad Greenway
- Easthampton Manhan Rail Trail
- The Manhan Rail Trail
- Norwottuck Bike Trail
- Northampton Bike Path

- The New Haven & Northampton Canal Greenway
- East Coast Greenway

Because each and every one of the above bike trails owes its existence to the New Haven & Northampton Canal System as originated in 1826, I choose the following rail-trail name for this book – the name came from the original canal as it evolved: New Haven & Northampton Canal Greenway

WHY WRITE A CANAL RAIL TRAIL GUIDE

I decided to write this guide because the old canal is slowly being destroyed.

Let me explain.

I knew nothing of the canal system as I was growing up in the 'Hill Towns' of Western Massachusetts (more commonly called 'The Berkshires' and more specifically in paper company owned housing developments called 'The Beehive'). When in High School, my parents moved to Westfield, Massachusetts. Next to our house was a big ditch, filled with trees, vines, standing water and almost anything else. A place you looked at but avoided.

Each day, on my way to school, I walked across the canal but did not know it. Sometime later, as an adult, I learned what the ditch was all about. . . . it was the remains of a canal system that at one time reached from Long Island Sound to the upper reaches of the Connecticut River. As time when on, I watched as developers flatten sections of the old canal to build houses, roads or to develop the area for pastures. The canal footprint is slowly being erased.

That's the real point of this book.

It always bothered me that history was being destroyed. Cars and people would drive by and never realize what once was. . . They passed by something that could have been another Erie Canal, something that still is in existence in New York but not in New England.

Today, how do you make people aware that the New Haven & Northampton Canal system existed? Of course, you could write a book. The problem was a book about a canal system filled with dimensions and technical facts might be boring to some and may not be read by many. The great thing about living a long time is you have time to do a lot of things, including walking New England sections of the Appalachian Trail, the Metacomet Trail, trails in the White Mountains of New Hampshire and other trails. I eventually hit upon the idea of writing a hiking and rail-trail guide about the ancient canal. Today, much of the original canal system became part of a much large railroad system driven by the invention of the steam engine.

So, the bottom line is this:

All royalties from this trail guide will be used to erect historic signs along the canal system to remind travelers that the canal system once existed. Local historical societies along the trail will determine where the signs will be placed and hopefully be responsible for its upkeep.

The Southwick Historical Society, Inc. in Southwick, Massachusetts will be the keeper of any and all revenue derived from the sales of this book. Several other historical societies along the route also maintain canal artifacts, displays and collections of photographs and other items donated by people interested in the canal.

DONATIONS CAN BE SENT TO:

Southwick Historical Society, Inc.
P.O. Box 323
Southwick, MA 01077
www.southwickhistoricalsociety.org

Some say the canal has a way of "sticking-in-your-claw and not letting loose". This is certainly true in my case (and I surmise several others notably Charles R. Harte, Raimon L Beard, Ruth S. Hummel and Carl E. Walter). As I noted above, when writing this book, I chose a rail-trail or bicycling format so that others can learn about the canal as well as have an enjoyable time discovering it as it exists today. If you want to get into the details and learn more about the works of these individuals and many others, go to the Selected Bibliography at the end of this book or, as I mentioned above, visit the Plainville Historical Society or other historic societies along this biking and hiking guide.

I hope you enjoy your bike ride through history. . .

BOB MADISON

NOTE: *A word about my watercolors. I framed each watercolor 'on location' to increase accuracy. That is, today, you can actually stand on location and visualize what it must have been like to be a bystander. For consistency, I made a model of a passenger packet boat and the boat's 'captain' was modeled after a real barge master or captain piloting a real canal barge in Chester, England. Because this book is in black and white, I've chosen colors suitable for insertion into this book. The watercolors were then run through a digital black & white program and photographed for insertion into my book.*

BIKE SAFETY, RULES AND REGULATIONS

HOW TO USE THIS RAIL TRAIL GUIDE

This guide is divided into 16 chapters or sections that represent the 16 towns the canal, railroad and rail trail travels through. And, each chapter or section is divided into the following descriptive groupings:

Common Names: Individual historical societies or rail trail groups together or individually championed the converting the rail beds into rail trails so they naturally named some of the trail after their community.

Route: The author arbitrarily chose a route or trailhead that started and stopped at or near the border of each town along the rail trail route. Under the 'parking heading', the hiker or biker can locate trailheads by using GPS addresses. In a few cases, two routes are indicated (Farmington, Westfield, Southampton & Northampton) to allow the hiker or biker to follow the original canal rather than the railroad.

Miles between trailheads are approximate and were based on my cyclometer and were rounded up or averaged. I also gave a time range for the slow pokes. If you are a high performance biker, these times become meaningless.

Significant Canal Features: Each town or village has a unique canal or rail trail feature. To make your ride interesting, the author has attempted to highlight the significance of each feature.

A **photo or picture** of historic significance in each community.

A **map of the rail trail** as it passes through a specific town or village. The map also shows where the canal is along with trailheads and route numbers.

⊗**TRAILHEAD instructions:** The New Haven & Northampton travels through 16 towns from beginning to end. Trail head locations were arbitrarily chosen near or on town borders. This means that parking may be on or near recognized parking lots but may also mean the hiker or biker may have to park on-street. Alternate parking areas are also indicated where possible. → Arrows are used to alert the hiker or biker when to change direction along with a brief set of instructions and sometimes an estimate of miles between specific locations. It is up to the reader of this guide to decide how and where they should carefully and safely park their vehicle, especially when parking 'on street'.

Instructions are for planning purpose only and are subject to change due to rail trail changes, traffic, construction, weather, etc. These changes may require the hiker or biker to alter the planned route. Plan accordingly and obey signs.

Parking Access: Approximate GPS addresses are noted for the convenience of the hiker of biker. ZIP Codes are also provided for ease when locating Trail Head parking. Please note that you, the person trying to find a parking spot, must use your own judgment as to where you can safely park.

Town history: A brief history of each town.

Canal history and a comment as to where the canal is located in relation to the rail trail.

Watercolor painting: An original watercolor painting by the watercolorist (author) depicting the packet passenger canal boat as it passes through a significant feature in each town.

Photographs: The intent of photographs in this book is to highlight significant items of interest as well as identify individuals who contributed to canal history.

Canal Railroad: A brief history of the railroad that the rail trail was built on.

Bicycle Repair / Rental Facility feature addresses and phone numbers for the biker in case repairs or advice is required.

Off Rail trail Excursions: A brief listing of nearby places to visit that may or may not require bicycles.

RAIL TRAIL GUIDE: The purpose of this guide is to give the hiker/biker a brief route description going both north or south. The **⊗TRAILHEAD instructions** gives specific details only traveling north.

AUTHOR'S COMMENTS

When hiking or bicycling the canal rail trail, don't be intimidated because you cannot actually hike or bike the actual canal (or railroad bed)! The original canal followed the contours of the earth (mountain ranges, valleys, hills, etc.). After all, it's a waterway and it must stay as flat as possible. Plus, today, much of the original canal is overgrown with trees or changed due to housing developments. When the steam engine was invented, the railway bed needed to be straight and true and it was not necessary to follow the curvature of the hills and valleys to make the waterway level. Some of it is hard to locate and some of it is on private property. All of it is historical and enjoyable because you are outside having a little fun and getting exercise.

Many parts of the rail trail are complete and labeled 'EAST COAST GREENWAY'. Other sections abruptly end and you are forced to hike or bike on busy streets. ***ALWAYS*** *use caution. The rail trail instructions in each chapter warn you to use extreme caution when traveling along these streets and byways!*

Construction and repairs constantly change the landscape as well as the bike and rail trail routes. Make your plans but don't be afraid to change them. This book should only be used as a general guide and a source of information about the canal, railroad and rail trail. Caution again is the byword when traveling along any rail trail or bike trail. Don't be afraid to ask fellow hikers or bikers for directions. Most will be more than happy to help you find your way.

FIRST AND FORMOST: USE COMMON SENSE

A helmet is your friend. Wear it. When in your car, you use your seat belt. When on a boat, you wear your life jacket. Remember, the other person might not be as conscientious as you are. A helmet is your friend. Make sure the helmet fits correctly. Loose enough so you can talk (place a few fingers under your chin strap to make sure the strap is not too tight). Get advice from your local bike shop.

Situational Awareness. Being aware of your surroundings and environment is something you learn in the military or athletics. Potholes, sticks or soft sand along the apron of the trail are obvious. A drunk driver or the sudden opening of a door when you are 'on street' is not so obvious. Never become isolated along long stretches. If you can, always bike with others. If alone or with a small group, sometimes it makes sense to safely rest along the trail until others come alongside; then, follow them until you are comfortable. Let someone know where you are going before you go.

Some Biking Rules complied by The League of American Bicyclists, the International Mountain Bike Association and others give guidance to bikers. Go to their website or other publications and follow their advice.

> •Make your intentions clear when you pass someone. Say "on your left" or, use a bell before passing. Use turn signals and check behind you before you pass someone.
>
> •Obey the law. Different areas have different rules. In general, bicyclists have to follow the same laws as motorists. Bicyclists also have the same right of way as motorists on public ways (refer to the rather lengthy

Massachusetts laws on bicycling at the end of this chapter).

•When on public roadways, bicycle on the same side as vehicles. Keep to the right shoulder of these roadways. Obey traffic signs, stop lights and speed regulations.

•Maintain control of your bicycle. Pay attention to little details and ride within your limits. If the trail is does not have a dividing lane separating traffic, the bicyclist traveling downhill should yield to the bicyclist traveling uphill. Cross railroad tracks at right angles.

•Children in child carriers must be protected from rear wheel spokes and be adequately secured in the carrier.

•Do no wear earphones and headsets or other electronic devices.

•Carry packages and other items in a basket, rack or trailer (not on your back).

•Rail trails are normally clearly marked. Stay off of other people's private property. Many parts of the trail go behind homes and businesses. Respect their privacy. Don't take shortcuts such as switchbacks.

•Be conspicuous. For your own safety, wear bright colors. Blinking lights attract attention. Use a white light in front, a red light in the rear and reflectors so others can see you. Include side reflectors.

•Plan ahead. The 'who, what, where and when' is a good way to think about any endeavor. Check the weather too.

•Take only pictures and leave only memories. . .

Animals: If you encounter animals on the Greenway, never scare them or startle them by an unannounced approach. No loud noises or sudden approaches. Give animals such as horses extra room and don't spook them. In case of doubt, ask the owner what to do (this goes for dogs and other animals). Dismount your bike if necessary. Your bike can also be used as a shield between you and an aggressive animal.

How to ride a bicycle: Adjust your seat so that the balls of your feet are on the pedals at the bottom of each stroke with your knees slightly bent. Your saddle or seat should be level with the earth (or top tube). And, don't overextend your back and arms when you reach your handlebars. If you are always uncomfortable, visit your local bike shop. Lastly, always maintain a constant gate or RPM by shifting gears. This will increase endurance. And, don't be afraid to rest every so often or walk your bike up a steep hill.

87 MILES. THAT'S THE LENGTH OF THE GREENWAY

Using data* from extreme bicyclist Bob Pac, a member of Westfield's Colombia Greenway, I calculated that the length of Bob's ride from the Yale was **85.1 miles** riding 'uphill' for **7.3 hours** or **11.7 miles per hour** from New Haven to Northampton (it's another 1.7 miles to the harbor). Of interest it took a canal boat to travel from New Haven's Harbor to Northampton about 24 hours traveling some 4 miles per hour (including waiting at least 5 minutes for each of the 60 locks to fill or empty throughout the system). An amazing ride for someone who was in his early seventies at the time of his ride!

Author's notes: *By combining two of Bob Pac rides (as recorded on MapMyRide**), the author pieced together the length of time and distance it takes to ride the greenway from the edge of the 'Farmington Canal Greenway' within the Yale University Campus to the 'Norwottuck Rail Trail' next to the Connecticut River in Northampton, MA. In summary, Bob Pac, a septuagenarian (the same age as this author), rode from Westfield MA to New Haven CT and back on August 29, 2014 for a [round trip] distance of 124.96 miles in 10 hours and 36 minutes and a second trip from Westfield MA to Northampton MA [one way] on October 8, 2015 for a distance of 22.55 miles in 2 hours and 12 minutes. There is an additional 1.7 miles and 14 minutes from the New Haven Harbor to the Yale University Campus; thus, the complete length of the New Haven & Northampton Canal Greenway including 'on street' downtown routes is 87 miles (give or take). The common published route of the canal length is 86 miles.*

***MapMyRide is a software program utilizing GPS and mapping techniques to document a bicyclists' ride.*

MAINTENANCE, GEAR AND REPAIRS

FIRST AND FORMOST:
Take a test ride before you go.

Check your equipment: "An ounce of prevention is worth a pound of cure". Checking tire pressure is a good start, especially if your bike has been sitting around for a while. Check your brakes. Keep your bike cleaned with mild soap (dish soap) and wash off with clean water; then, lubricate your chain and wheel hubs after you dry everything off. To be a little more specific, wipe your chain off with a clean rag to take off the grime (including the derailleurs and crank gears); then, get lubrication advice from your bike shop.

Essential gear list: If you think small, you should be able to put some or all of your short term gear into a small saddle bag. Avoid back packs because they increase your center of gravity. Trails and bikeways along The New Haven & Northampton Canal Greenway Rail Trail will not take you very far from civilization. In fact, most of the time you will be very close to access points along the trail easily reachable by car. Your list all depends on how far you are away from your vehicle or repair shop. The short list:

•Tire pump
•Patch kit
•Tire levers or screw driver and an adjustable wrench.
•Small rag
•Bicycle lock

Other gear for your consideration: If you are on the Greenway for long distances, you may want to have access to some or all of the following items:

•Helmet (always wear this essential gear)
•Water & high energy food is at the top of the list
•Light/flashers
•Air gauge
•Allen wrenches
•Adjustable or crescent wrenches
•Multitool

- Chain rivet tool and spare chain links
- Spoke wrench
- Oil and lubricant
- Tire valve caps
- Spare tires & tubes
- Nuts & bolts
- Duct tape
- Money/credit card
- First-aid kit
- Rain gear
- Spare clothing
- Hat & gloves
- Sunscreen, lip balm and sunglasses
- GPS, cell phone, compass and bike computer
- The list goes on-and-on

† If you really want to get into the 'nitty-gritty' of rules and regulations, the following quote (italicized by the author) comes from Massachusetts General Laws, Chapter 85, Section 11B:

Every person operating a bicycle upon a way, as defined in section one of chapter ninety, shall have the right to use all public ways in the commonwealth except limited access or express state highways where signs specifically prohibiting bicycles have been posted, and shall be subject to the traffic laws and regulations of the commonwealth and the special regulations contained in this section, except that: (1) the bicycle operator may keep to the right when passing a motor vehicle which is moving in the travel lane of the way, (2) the bicycle operator shall signal by either hand his intention to stop or turn; provided, however, that signals need not be made continuously and shall not be made when the use of both hands is necessary for the safe operation of the bicycle, and (3) bicycles may be ridden on sidewalks outside business districts when necessary in the interest of safety, unless otherwise directed by local ordinance. A person operating a bicycle on the sidewalk shall yield the right of way to pedestrians and give an audible signal before overtaking and passing any pedestrian.

Operators of bicycles shall be subject to the following regulations:

(1) Bicyclists riding together shall not ride more than 2 abreast but, on a roadway with more than 1 lane in the direction of travel, bicyclists shall ride within a single lane. Nothing in this clause shall relieve a bicyclist of the duty to facilitate overtaking as required by Section 2 of Chapter 89.

(2)(i) The operator shall ride only upon or astride a permanent and regular seat attached to the bicycle; a passenger shall ride only upon or astride a permanent and regular seat attached to the bicycle or to a trailer towed by the bicycle.

(ii) The operator shall not transport another person between the ages of one to four years, or weighing forty pounds or less, on a bicycle, except in a "baby seat", so-called, attached to the bicycle, in which such other person shall be able to sit upright; provided, however, that such seat is equipped with a harness to hold such other person securely in the seat and that protection is provided against the feet or hands of such person hitting the spokes of the wheel of the bicycle; or upon or astride a seat of a tandem bicycle equipped so that the other person can comfortably reach the handlebars and pedals. The operator shall not transport any person under the age of one year on said bicycle.

(iii) Any person 16 years of age or younger operating a bicycle or being carried as a passenger on a bicycle on a public way, bicycle path or on any other public right-of-way shall wear a helmet. Said helmet shall fit the person's head, shall be secured to the person's head by straps while the bicycle is being operated, and shall meet the standards for helmets established by the United States Consumer Product Safety Commission. These requirements shall not apply to a passenger if the passenger is in an enclosed trailer or other device which adequately holds the passenger in place and protects the passenger's head from impact in an accident.

(iv) A violation of clause (ii) or (iii) shall not be used as evidence of contributory negligence in any civil action.

(3) The operator shall give an audible warning whenever necessary to insure safe operation of the bicycle; provided, however, the use of a siren or whistle is prohibited.

(4) The operator shall park his bicycle upon a way or a sidewalk in such a manner as not to obstruct vehicular or pedestrian traffic.

(5) The operator shall not permit the bicycle to be drawn by any other moving vehicle. The operator shall not tow any other vehicle or person, except that bicycle trailers properly attached to the bicycle which allow for firm control and braking may be used.

(6) The operator shall not carry any package, bundle or article except in or on a basket, rack, trailer or other device designed for such purposes. The operator shall keep at least one hand upon the handlebars at all times.

(7) Every bicycle operated upon a way shall be equipped with a braking system to enable the operator to bring the bicycle traveling at a speed of fifteen miles per hour to a smooth, safe stop within thirty feet on a dry, clean, hard, level surface.

(8) During the period from one-half hour after sunset to one-half hour before sunrise, the operator shall display to the front of his bicycle a lamp emitting a white light visible from a distance of at least five hundred feet, and to the rear of said bicycle either a lamp emitting a red light, or a red reflector visible for not less than six hundred feet when directly in front of lawful lower beams of headlamps on a motor vehicle. A generator powered lamp which emits light only when the bicycle is moving shall meet the requirements of this clause.

(9) During the period from one-half hour after sunset to one-half hour before sunrise, the operator shall display on each pedal of his bicycle a reflector, or around each of his ankles reflective material visible from the front and rear for a distance of six hundred feet, and reflectors or reflective material, either on said bicycle or on the person of the operator, visible on each side for a distance of six hundred feet, when directly in front of lawful lower beams of headlamps of a motor vehicle. This clause shall not prohibit a bicycle or its operator to be equipped with lights or reflectors in addition to those required by clauses (8) and (9).

(10) No bicycle shall be operated upon a way with handlebars so raised that the operator's hands are above his shoulders while gripping them. Any alteration to extend the fork of a bicycle from the original design and construction of the bicycle manufacturer is prohibited.

(11) The operator of a bicycle shall report any accident involving either personal injury or property damage in excess of one hundred dollars, or both, to the police department in the city or town in which the accident occurred.

Any federal product safety standards relating to bicycles which are more stringent than the requirements of clauses (7) through (10), inclusive, shall supersede said requirements.

Competitive bicycle races may be held on public ways, provided that such races are sponsored by or in cooperation with recognized bicycle organizations and, provided further, that the sponsoring organization shall have obtained the approval of the appropriate police department or departments. Special regulations regarding the movement of bicycles during such races, or in training for races, including, but not limited to, permission to ride abreast, may be established by agreement between the police department and the sponsoring organization.

Violations of any provision of this section except violations of subclause (iii) of clause (2) shall be punished by a fine of not more than twenty dollars. The parent or guardian of any person under age eighteen shall not authorize or knowingly permit any such person to violate any of the provisions of this section. A bicycle operated by a person under the age of eighteen in violation of this section may be impounded by the police department, or in a town which has no police department, by the selectmen, for a period not to exceed fifteen days. A violation of any provision of this section by a minor under the age of eighteen shall not affect any civil right or liability nor shall such violation be considered a criminal offense.

SOURCE NOTES

- Massachusetts General Laws, Chapter 85, Section 11B:
- The League of American Bicyclists
- The International Mountain Bike Association

NEW HAVEN AND NORTHAMPTON CANAL GREENWAY

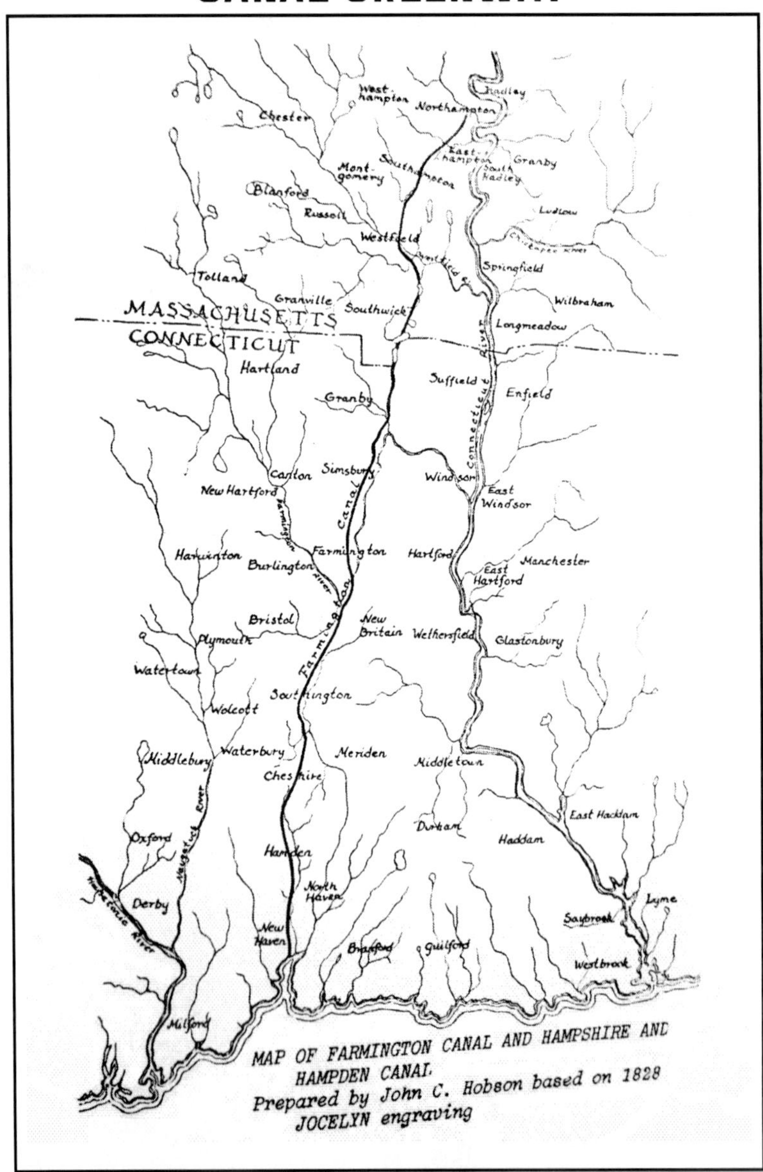

MAP OF FARMINGTON CANAL AND HAMPSHIRE AND HAMPDEN CANAL

Prepared by John C. Hobson based on 1828 JOCELYN engraving

PROFILES OF ELEVATIONS
A REPRESENTATION

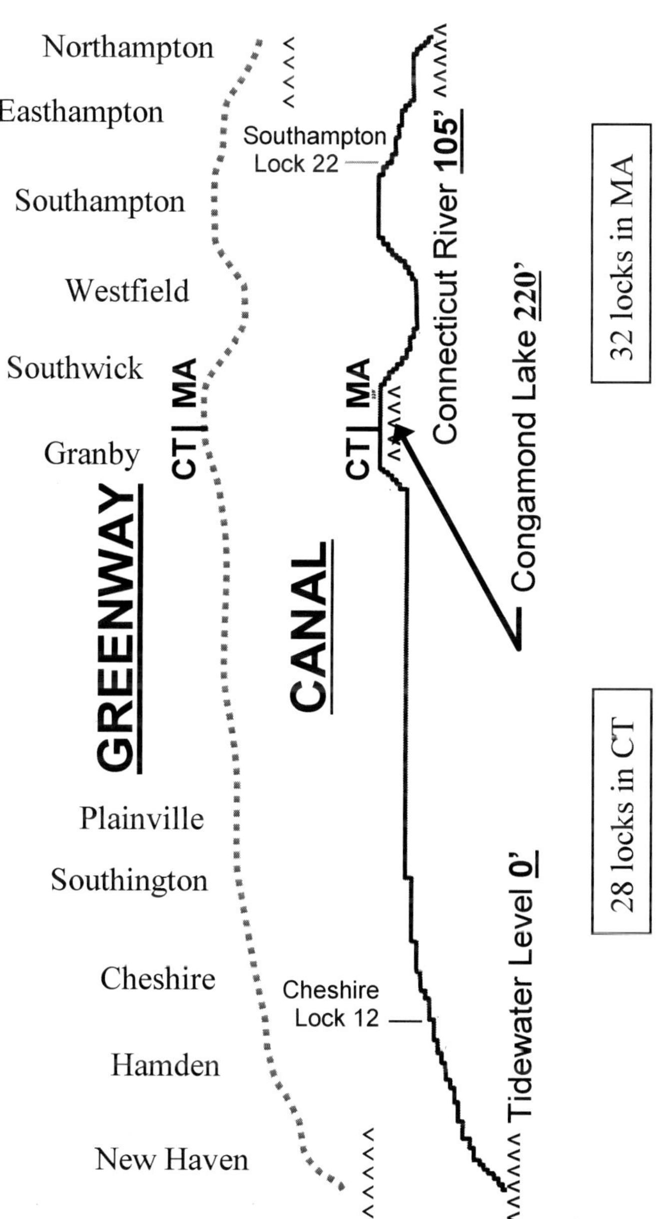

NOTES

SECTION 1: NEW HAVEN
(FARMINGTON CANAL HERITAGE TRAIL)

Common Names: East Coast Greenway, Farmington Canal Heritage Trail, Farmington Canal Greenway, The Farmington Canal and includes parts of the Vision Trail.

Route: New Haven Long Wharf Dr. to Putnam Ave. in Hamden.
Total Distance: 4.5 miles or 30 - 60 minutes depending upon downtown traffic.

Ride Details: Skill level is easy to moderate. The trail goes from the waterfront through Yale Campus. Mostly mixture of city/bicycle trails. Some bike paths are in heavy traffic areas. Elevation gain is minimal. According to newspaper reports, caution must be exercised while bicycling in some parts of New Haven.

Significant Canal Features: Ocean access to canal started at the Harbor Basin (harbor or port was built in 1827 and the basin was filled a long time ago); locks 22 – 27 are not visible but some of the canal depressions on Yale University Campus are visible.

The Farmington Canal Greenway will ultimately connect the Vision Trail from the New Haven Harbor past Yale University north & south along the abandoned canal and railroad right-of-way. The East Coast Greenway Alliance links many of the rail-trails from Florida to Canada.

NEW HAVEN RAIL TRAIL MAP

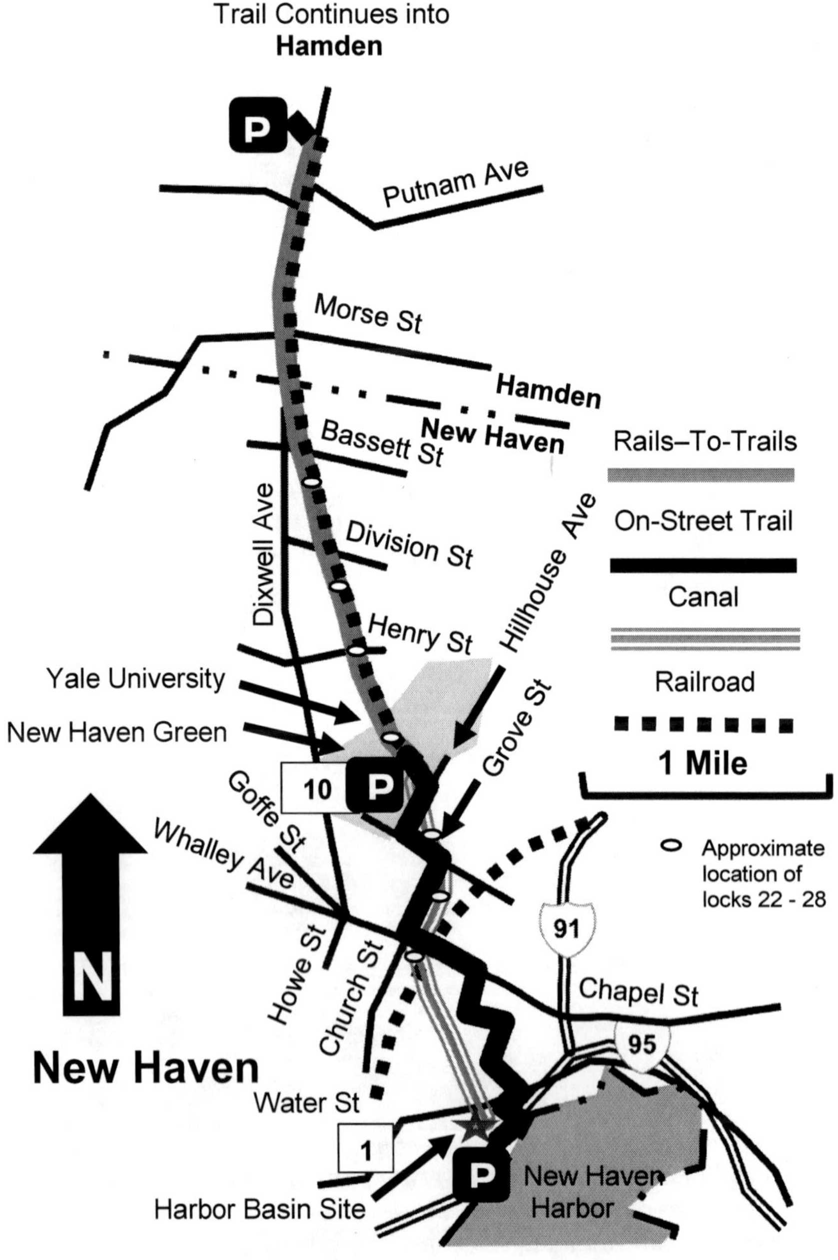

FARMINGTON CANAL GREENWAY

NEW HAVEN RAIL TRAIL

Rail Trail:

⊗**TRAILHEAD:** New Haven, CT. Off Interstate 95, Follow GPS and park at Long Wharf Park on Long Wharf Dr. (off street available). You are on the Vision Trail.

> *NOTICE: Until New Haven's Vision Trail is completed, bikers can follow my suggested busy on-street Brewer St route through downtown New Haven and onto the FCHT off Hillhouse Ave.*

↑ Bike northeast 0.2 mi on Long Wharf Drive.

← Turn left onto 'brick lined' Vision Trail (Canal Dock Rd) [under I95] until you reach Sargent Dr. in 0.2 mi.

→ Bike across Sargent Dr., take a right and follow Sargent Dr. onto Brewery St 0.3 mi. NOTE: If Vision Trail disappears due to construction, continue to Water St/US-1 0.2 mi.

You are now at historic Basin Wharf [see CANAL HISTORY on following pages]. *The wharf is long gone. The original canal follows the railroad tracks north for a while. Across the tracks is North Haven Union Station AMTRAK Station.*

← Turn left onto Water St/US-1 0.2 mi.

→ Take your second right onto Union St 0.2 miles or about 4 minutes (with the Union Street Dog Park on your left) to Chapel St.

← Turn left onto Chapel St and bicycle over the train bridge to Church St 0.3 mi.

→ Turn right at Church St 0.3 mi. (on your left is New Haven Green and on your right are Federal Buildings) continue to Grove St [NOTE: because of one-way streets, if southbound, take a right onto Temple St 0.4 mi. past Grove St to Chapel St]

← You will soon take a left onto Grove St 0.2 mi.

→ When you see Hillhouse Ave turn right [onto Hillhouse Ave]. (Yale University Campus has many bike paths in this area). Just up the road on Hillhouse (one way) about 0.1 mi. turn left onto Farmington Canal Heritage Trail (FCHT). Access the FCHT from several streets including Hillhouse, Trumbull or Prospect. *(NOTE: various accesses at the Farmington Canal Greenway Park).* Route parallels Canal St & Lock St for a short time.

↑ Continue on the FCHT for 2.4 miles north or about 14 minutes until you arrive at Putnam Ave (Putnam Ave Overpass: On your right is the Whitney Lake area and as you leave the FCHT, you travel over the ancient lock 21).

← To your left is Putnam Place Mall and parking. 0.1 mi.

⊗**TRAILHEAD:** Hamden, CT. Parking at the shopping malls at the intersection of Putnam Ave and Dixwell Ave.

DIRECTIONS SOUTH? Go to the Rail Trail Guide at the end of this chapter.

PARKING ACCESS:

New Haven, CT

- **Trailhead GPS:** 350 Long Wharf Dr, ZIP 06511. Parking on Long Wharf Dr. (on-street parking might be available in several areas along Long Wharf Drive including covered garages). The general area under US-95 is industrial and was at one time a fairground.

- Another good place to park for free is around the Yale Campus. Take Exit 3 on US-91 onto Trumbull St driving to Hillhouse Ave and on-street parking (look for on-street or garage parking in the area).

- On-street parking throughout the city as well as private parking lots.

- On-street parking on Hillhouse Ave.

Hamden, CT

- **Trailhead GPS:** 1230 Dixwell Ave, ZIP 06247. Parking at the shopping malls on the intersection of Putnam Ave and Dixwell Ave.

- Parking next to FCHT/near Quinnipiac University, 3450 Whitney Ave/US-10.

NEW HAVEN HISTORY

New Haven was settled by English Puritans in 1638 originally calling their settlement 'Quinnipiac', the name of the Indian tribe (belonging to the Algonquian tribe) occupying the land at that time. Dutch navigator Adriaen Block passed this area in 1614. In 1664, King Charles I punished fleeing judges who settled in the area because they condemned the king to death. The king retaliated by absorbing the independent colony into the Hartford ruled Connecticut Colony. New Haven and Hartford were co-capitals of Connecticut from 1701 to 1873. Yale College (now Yale University) moved to New Haven in 1716. The ships of New Haven, then and now, are known for their sea trading abilities.

During the Revolutionary War, the British troops burned and looted the city.

In the early years, New Haven was known for the Winchester Rifle, cigars, bicycles, watches, standardization of manufacturing, vulcanization of rubber and many other notable goods. Today, New Haven is a modern Long Island Sound city which continues to revitalize and renew itself.

NEW HAVEN CANAL HISTORY

Where's the canal? The canal that once existed near the New Haven Harbor is long gone. It is buried under tons of rubble (see map). It is not until you get off the city streets and onto the Farmington Canal Heritage Trail (just north of the Yale University Campus) that you are actually on the canal again.

Canal History: New Haven is where it all happened; that is, many years ago, New Haven and Hartford annually alternated being the capital city of Connecticut. Hartford had the Connecticut River and New Haven needed a similar connection into the interior. Thus, on January 29, 1822, the representatives of seventeen towns met in Farmington to discuss the merits of a canal route through their villages. On May, 1822, the Farmington Canal Company was chartered (readers can refer to the Selected Bibliography in the back of this book for all the details). Back then, other than the Connecticut River, the only way interior commerce could be conducted was by way of dirt roads or pathways: dusty and rutted in the summer, muddy when it rained or frozen or impassable in the winter. Plus, travelers on the better roads or turnpikes had numerous tolls to contend with.

Next to the canal on New Haven's Wooster Street, was a grist mill, powered by canal water. The grist mill (called 'City Mill"), built by Captain Roland, was located near Lock 28; became very famous and "stood until the construction of the railroad station between Wooster and Chapel Streets. New Haven had eight locks (heading south, Locks 22 to 28) somewhat spaced evenly as you travel to the Hamden/New Haven border. A 'busy' basin area was located at the end/beginning of the Farmington Canal Heritage Trail somewhere between Temple Street and Whitney Street where the site of Hillhouse Basin, Lock 26 and a canal repair shop once existed. The basin was actually a walled dam extension inside the harbor and next to shore. It was designed to keep out tidal fluctuations.

When completed, the entire length of the canal was some 86 miles with 28 locks in Connecticut and 32 locks in Massachusetts.

The major source for canal water was a feeder dam in Farmington which supplied water all the way from Granby to New Haven.

By bicycle, on the Vision Trail and near Sargent Dr. and Brewery ST, stop and look toward the harbor to see where the Historic Harbor Basin (the place where canal boats loaded and unloaded goods) once was. A watercolor painting by the author will give the reader an idea of what the harbor looked like in 1839 when the slave ship *Amistad* was docked along Basin Wharf. The basin is on the right side of the watercolor painting. Follow the on-street route to Yale University and pick up the Farmington Heritage Canal Trail which follows the original canal route. North of Yale University, the original canal follows the contours of the terrain, just west of the FCHT (see map).

Above is a watercolor image of the slave ship 'Amistad' as it might have appeared in 1839. A canal packet or passenger boat is on the right side of the painting. The canal boat is pictured outside the basin (an enclosed holding area) in New Haven Harbor. Once inside the basin, the boat is at the correct elevation to enter Lock 28 as it makes its journey into the interior of New England. The author invites the reader to get aboard and follow his excursion boat north. Watercolor by Robert R. Madison

Canal boat PIONEER off Grand Avenue in New Haven. A typical freighter was 70' long and 11' wide. Freighters carried the heavy loads such as coal, lumber and bricks. The passenger boat or packet was about 60' to 65' long and 11' wide. It took about 24 hours to travel from New Haven to Northampton. – New Haven Colonial Historical Society.

CANAL RAILROAD

Where's the railroad? The old Canal Railroad had its start in New Haven.

Railroad History: In fact, in the early days, the Round Table, Engine House and Passenger Depot were located between Hillside and Temple just north of Grove St (this is where I show the start of the iron railroad tracks). At the intersection of Hillside and The Farmington Canal Heritage Trail, the rail tracks cross the old canal on their way north following today's rail-trail. Much later, lines south to Chapel connected to New Haven Station. "Back in the day", Canal Dock Rd was a wharf that projected out into the New Haven Harbor. Railroad tracks were laid on Canal Dock and the tracks led where the wharf once was past the current intersection of Brewer St with the tracks leading roughly from Canal Dock Rd traveling northward. Construction of The New Haven & Northampton RR (NH&N) began in New Haven through the village of Hampden ending in Cheshire in 1847. The route chosen was along the original old Farmington Canal right-of-way (and some sections of the old Cheshire Turnpike). Just north of Yale University, where Brewster St and the FCHT cross, you will see several hundred feet of switch tracks.

Bicycling enthusiast inspecting original railroad tracks next to the Farmington Canal Heritage Trail near the Yale Campus in New Haven.

To be historically correct, the New Haven and Northampton Railroad, reorganized itself as New Haven and Northampton Company in 1847 (Joseph Sheffield was the largest stockholder). Tracks loosely followed the current rail-trail path along its 86 mile route to Northampton, MA. Between 1848 and 1869 the route was operated by other railroad companies including the New Haven & Northampton RR, the New York & Northampton RR, the New Haven RR, the Penn Central RR and Boston & Maine RR and lastly CONRAIL. The railway was finally abandoned in 1987.

BICYCLE REPAIR AND RENTAL FACILITIES

College Street Cycles
252 College St
New Haven, CT 06510
203 865-2724
www.collegestreetcycles@gmail.com.

The Devil's Gear Bike Shop
151 Orange St
New Haven, CT 06510
203 773-9288
http://thedevilsgear.com/

D Anielios Amity New Haven Bicycles
433 Chapel St.
New Haven, CT 06511
203 624-6734

OFF RAIL TRAIL EXCURSIONS

(Excursions may or may not require bicycles)

1. **New Haven City Hall and New Haven Green**
165 Church St, New Haven
203 946-8200
www.cityofnewhaven.com

2. Yale University Visitor Center
149 Elm St.
New Haven
www.yale.edu

3. University of New Haven
300 Boston Post Rd.
West Haven, CT
800 342-5864
www.newhaven.edu

4. Amistad Memorial
165 Church St. (in front of New Haven City Hall)
New Haven
www.amistadcommitteeinc.org

5. Grove Street Cemetery
227 Grove St.
New Haven, CT
www.grovestreetcemetery.org

6. New Haven Museum
114 Whitney Ave.
New Haven
203 562-4183
www.newhavenmuseum.org

7. Fort Nathan Hall and Black Rock Fort
36 Woodward Ave.
New Haven
203 946-6970
www.fort-nathan-hale.org

8. Schooner Quinnipiack, Long Wharf pier
389 Long Wharf Dr.
New Haven
203 865-1737
www.schoonerinc.org

9. **New Haven Museum & Historical Society**
114 Whitney Ave.
New Haven CT
203 562-4183
newhavenmuseum.org

10. **Yale Peabody Museum of Natural History**
170 Whitney Ave.
New Haven CT
203 432-3776
peabody.events@yale.edu

Marsh Botanic Gardens
227 Mansfield St.

Long Wharf Park
Long Wharf Dr.

Fairmont Park
399 Quinnipiac Ave.

New Haven Green
202 Temple St.

Shepard & Huntington
Huntington St.

Edgewood Park
Whalley Ave

Wooster Square Historic District
2 Wooster Pl.

Oyster Point Historic District
Howard Ave

RAIL TRAIL GUIDE

NORTH

MILES N		HEADING SOUTH MILES S
4.6	⊗ **TRAILHEAD** @ Hamden, CT, Putnam Avenue	0
	↑ Putnam Ave/Dixwell Ave area to Farmington Canal Heritage Trail (FCHT).	0.1
	→ FCHT to Hillhouse Ave	2.4
	→ Hillhouse Ave 'walking bike' on sidewalk south a short distance onto ← left on Trumball St	0.1
	← Left onto Trumball St	0.1
	→ Right unto Temple St	0.5
	← Left onto Chapel St	0.5
	→ Right onto Olive St	0.2
	← Left onto Water St./US-1	0.1
	→ Take your first right onto Brewery St	0.1
	↑ Vision Trail (along Sargent Dr) takes a quick left with Canal Dock Rd on your left.	0.2
	← Left on Vision Trail (Canal Dock Rd) to Long Wharf Dr	0.1
	→ Long Wharf Dr (Vision Trail) bike south to Long Wharf Park where you take a left to end your 88 mile bike ride from Northampton, MA. Congratulations!	0.2
0.1	→ FCHT near Putname Ave/Dixwell Ave Shopping Malls.	
2.4	← leave FCHT on your left before overpass to Putname Ave/Dixwell Ave	
0.1	→ Hillhouse Ave area to Farminton Canal Heritage Trail (FCHT).	
0.1	← Grove St. to right ont Hillhouse Ave	
0.3	→ Church St to left on Grove St	
0.3	← Left on Chapel St to right onto Church St.	
0.2	→ Water St to second right onto Union St to left on Chapel St	
0.2	← Turn left onto Water Street/US-1 0.2 mi.	
0.2	← Sargent Dr to Brewery looping left.	
0.3	→ Bike to Sargent Dr	
0.2	← Turn left onto Canal Dock Rd	
0.2	↑ Long Wharf Dr (Vision Trail) bike northwest to Canal Dock Rd	
0	⊗ **TRAILHEAD** @ New Haven, CT, Long Wharf Park	4.6

HEADING NORTH

SOUTH

SECTION 2: HAMDEN
(FARMINGTON CANAL TRAIL)

Common Names: East Coast Greenway, Farmington Canal Trail, Farmington Canal Greenway and Farmington Canal Heritage Trail.

Route: Putnam Ave, Hamden to North Brooksvale Rd, Cheshire.

Total Distance: 10.3 miles or 60 to 90 minutes

Ride Details: Skill level is easy to moderate. Elevation gain is minimal.

Significant Canal Features: Locks 13 – 21 are within Hamden's borders. Just south of Shepard Rd (41W 26′ 8.1°, -72° 54′ 30.88°) the remains of Lock 14 can be seen in the ditch next to the bike path (see photo). If you look toward 3908 Whitney Ave this was where the lockkeeper lived. All other locks disappeared over time. Many were built of wood rather than stone. Shepard Brook Culvert and Eaton Brook Culvert were two 8′ stone arches allowing canal barges to pass over watery streams. Riders will be able to read about the canal from the several informative signs posted along the route.

Bicyclist on the canal towpath or rail-trail with Shepard Road, Hamden, CT in the background, the canal is on the left in the photo and Lock 14 Lockkeeper's House (unseen) to the right.

HAMDEN RAIL TRAIL MAP

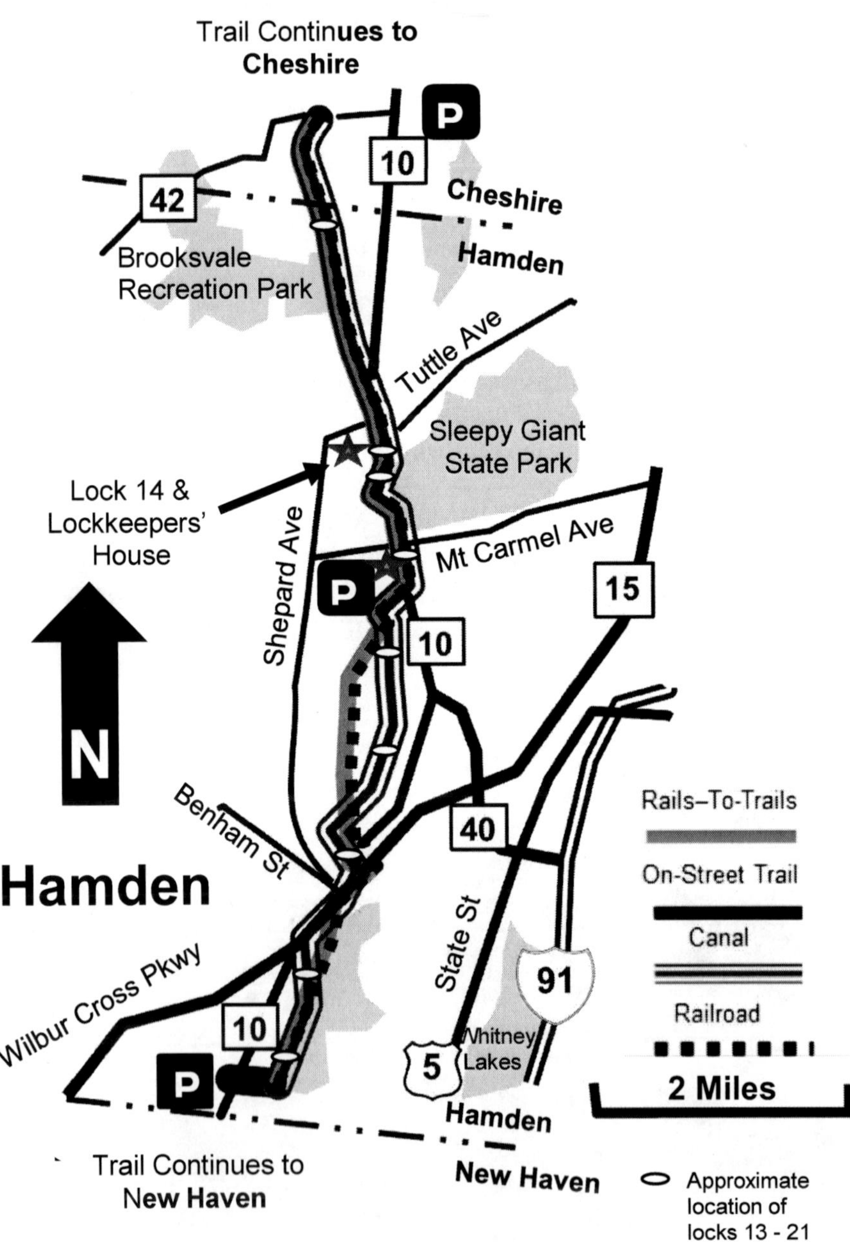

FARMINGTON CANAL TRAIL

HAMDEN RAIL TRAIL

Rail Trail:

⊗**TRAILHEAD:** Hamden, CT. From Parking at the shopping malls on the intersection of Putnam Ave and Dixwell Ave.

← Head toward Putnam Ave 0.1 mi.

← Turn left onto the Farmington Canal Heritage Trail (FCHT).

↑Travel northeast on FCHT 2.7 mi. to arrive at the CT-15/Wilbur Cross Pkwy pedestrian overpass.

↑Continue northeast 7.5 mi arriving at Lock 12, Farmington Canal Park. This is a long and well used section of the bike path.

⊗**TRAILHEAD:** Cheshire. CT. Park at the Farmington Canal Park. CT-42/455 North Brooksvale Rd, Cheshire, CT. This is where the restored Lock 12 is located.

DIRECTIONS SOUTH? Go to the Rail Trail Guide at the end of this chapter

PARKING ACCESS.

Hamden, CT

- **Trailhead GPS:** 1230 Dixwell Ave, ZIP 06247. Parking at the shopping malls on the intersection of Putnam Ave and Dixwell Ave.

- Parking next to FCHT/near Quinnipiac University, 3450 Whitney Ave/US 10.

- Nearby shopping parking at the intersection of Shepard Rd and 3950 Whitney Ave/US-10 near the FCHT and the remains of Lock 14.

Cheshire, CT

•Trailhead GPS: 455 North Brooksvale Rd, ZIP 06410. Park at the Farmington Canal Park. CT-42/455 North Brooksvale Rd, Cheshire, CT.

HAMDEN HISTORY

Hamden is now as then a small community that was settled in early eighteen hundreds as 'Windham Village'. The first settlers were mainly farmers. They settled the land by cutting trees and clearing the land for their homes and outbuildings.

According to the town's website, "the settlers needed oxen to plow and cows for milk, butter, cheese and meat. Their diet also included fish, turkey, deer, rabbit, duck and dove as well as fruits, vegetables and nuts. The work on the farm was hard. The entire family worked day and night." In 1786, the Town of Hamden was incorporated.

Today, Hamden is less dependent on farming; however, "Preserving open space and controlled, responsible development are 2 of the town's goals." The towns motto is "Land Of The Sleeping Giant" because on Metacomet Ridge, a prominent mountain outcrop features a slumbering human figure.

HAMDEN CANAL HISTORY

Where's the canal? The canal faithfully follows the rail-trail just north and south of Hamden; however, in the middle, it veers back and forth. Just south of Putnam Ave (near Lock 21), the canal is sandwiched between the rail-trail and US-10/Dixwell Ave until it reaches CT-15/Wilbur Cross Pkwy and then veers east loosely following US-10/Whitney Ave until just south of Mount Carmel Ave where the canal again loosely follows US-10/Whitney Ave on its way to the Cheshire border (see map).

Canal History: The village of Hamden had nine Locks (Locks 13 to 21 traveling south [NOTE: the trail instructions track north]). Locks were numbered north to south where Lock 1 was just south of the Massachusetts border at Congamond Lake. On July 4th, 1825, ground was first broken in Hamden toward the canal's journey to Long Island Sound. All in all, there were 28 locks in Connecticut and 32 locks in

Massachusetts which lifted northbound canal boats 310′ and lowered them 213′ until finally reaching the Connecticut River in Northampton, MA after traveling some 86 miles. Hamden's Lock 14, the remains of which can be seen from the rail trail, is much quoted because a farmer living nearby, acting as a lockkeeper, would operate Lock 14 when a canal boat captain would blow his horn. Today, the rail-trail/tow path travels between the brownstone Lock 14 and the farmer's house next to the trail. About two-thirds of the locks in Connecticut were in Hamden and New Haven (just south of Shepard Rd crossing). Land in this area sloped sharply toward New Haven Harbor requiring additional locks. Of some interest, many locks were made of wood which rotted quickly and had to be repaired frequently. The canals themselves were 20′ wide at the bottom and 34′ to 36′ wide at the surface. In addition, the towpath was at least 10′ wide and not more than 5′ above the water's surface. The opposite bank from the towpath could not be less than 2′ above the water's surface. Also of interest, if you follow the cut of any canal as it winds its way around the contours of a hill or mountain, you will observe the builders moved uphill dirt and deposited the dirt opposite the towpath to create the 10′ towpath bed.

Culverts, on the other hand were stone structures that allowed canal boats to travel 'over' brooks. Hamden had three notable culverts: the Eaton Brook Culvert; the Pardees Brook Culvert and the Shepard Brook Culvert.

HAMDEN RAIL TRAIL

Lock 14 Lockkeepers' house. Watercolor by Robert R. Madison

This picture shows the unrestored Lock 14 in the foreground. Between the lock and the Lockkeeper's house is the rail-trail which was originally a 10' wide towpath and later became the railroad bed.

CANAL RAILROAD

Where's the railroad? The rail tracks and the Farmington Heritage Canal Trail are one and the same (except for a few jogs now and then).

Railroad History: Construction of The New Haven & Northampton RR (NH&N) began in New Haven through the village of Hamden ending in Cheshire in 1847. The route chosen was along the original old Farmington Canal right-of-way (and some sections of the old Cheshire Turnpike). For the most part, the rail trail follows the original rail road tracks (original tow path). A railroad depot was built in Hamden in 1872 which caused an economic boom for the village. Between 1848 and 1869 the route was operated by other railroad companies including the New Haven & Northampton RR, the New York & Northampton RR, the New Haven RR, the Penn Central RR and Boston & Maine RR and lastly CONRAIL. The railway was finally abandoned in 1987.

The Canal Line was a popular nickname for the New Haven & Northampton Railroad years ago. Signs like this appear along the rail trail. Also, along the trail, the rider passes original brick railroad buildings (noted below).

The brick Mt Carmel Station in the foreground was built by the New Haven & Northampton RR in 1980. In the background is another brick building once used to house freight (on the Farmington Canal Trail near the intersection of Sherman Ave and Whitney Ave/US-10).

BICYCLE REPAIR AND RENTAL

Cheshire Cycle
3550 Whitney Ave
Hamden, CT
203 5320
http://www.cheshirecycle.com/

Cheshire Cycle & Repair
Serving the Cheshire Area
203 250-9996
http://www.cheshirecycle.com/

OFF RAIL TRAIL EXCURSIONS

(Excursions may or may not require bicycles)

1. Hamden Town Hall
2750 Dixwell Ave
Hamden, CT 06518
203 287-7112
www.hamptonct.org

2. Farmington Canal Linear Park
14 miles of biking, hiking beginning in Hamden and ending in Cheshire. Parking available on Todd St, Sherman Ave, Brooksvale Park and Connolly Pkwy. 203 287-2579

3. The Lock-Keeper's House
(41.435439 -72.909153)
The Lockkeeper's House was located next to the remains of Lock 14, The Lockkeeper was within walking distance of his house. This allowed the captain of the canal boat to signal with his horn.

4. Miller Memorial Central Library
2901 Dixwell Ave
Hamden, CT 06518
203 287-2682
www.Hamdenlibrary.org

5. Hamden Historical Society
Contact Miller Memorial Central Library
www.Hamdenhistoricalsociety.wordpress.com

Brundage Community Branch
Head 0.1 mi north on 91 Circular Ave from Putnam Ave and Dixwell Ave

Hamden Memorial Recreational Park; Beth El Memorial Park
41 Warner St

East Rock Park
41 Cold Spring St

RAIL TRAIL GUIDE

NORTH

MILES N		HEADING SOUTH MILES S
10.3	⊗ **TRAILHEAD @** Cheshire, CT, N. Brooksvale Road	0
	↑ The Farmington Canal Park parking lot, CT-42/455 N Brooksvale Rd, to Lock 12.	0.1
	↑ Cheshire Lock 12 to CT-15/Wilbur Cross Pkwy overpass.	7.5
	↑ CT-15/Wilbur Cross Pkwy Overpass to Putnam Rd intersection.	2.7
	→ right onto Putnam Rd intersection to Putnam Ave/Dixwell Ave parking.	0.1
0.1	↑ Lock 12 to the Farmington Canal Park parking lot.	
7.5	↑ CT-15/Wilbur Cross Pkwy overpass to Cheshire Lock 12 before arriving the Farmington Canal Park parking lot.	
2.7	↑ Farmington Canal Heritage Trail entrance to CT-15/Wilbur Cross Pkwy pedestrian Overpass.	
0.1	← Putnam Ave/Dixwell Ave parking to rail trail entrance.	
0	⊗ **TRAILHEAD** @ Hampden, CT, Putnam Avenue	10.3
HEADING NORTH		

SOUTH

NOTES

SECTION 3: CHESHIRE
(FARMINGTON CANAL HERITAGE TRAIL)

Common Names: East Coast Greenway and Farmington Canal Heritage Trail.

Route: North Brooksvale Rd, Cheshire to Canal St, Cheshire.

Total Distance: 6.4 miles or 40 – 60 minutes

Ride Details: Skill level is easy to moderate. Rail trail elevation gain is minimal. Route travels through busy Cheshire streets with moderate elevation.

Significant Canal Features: Locks 10 – 12 are within Cheshire's borders. Lock 12 along with its Lock House has been fully restored. Some vehicle parking exits along the trail with places to rest and take pictures. Lock 12 is an excellent example of what a stoned lined, wooden gate operational lock looked like back in eighteen hundreds. West Cheshire had its own port called 'Beachport'.

Lots of activity on the Cheshire rail-trail in early fall!

CHESHIRE RAIL TRAIL MAP

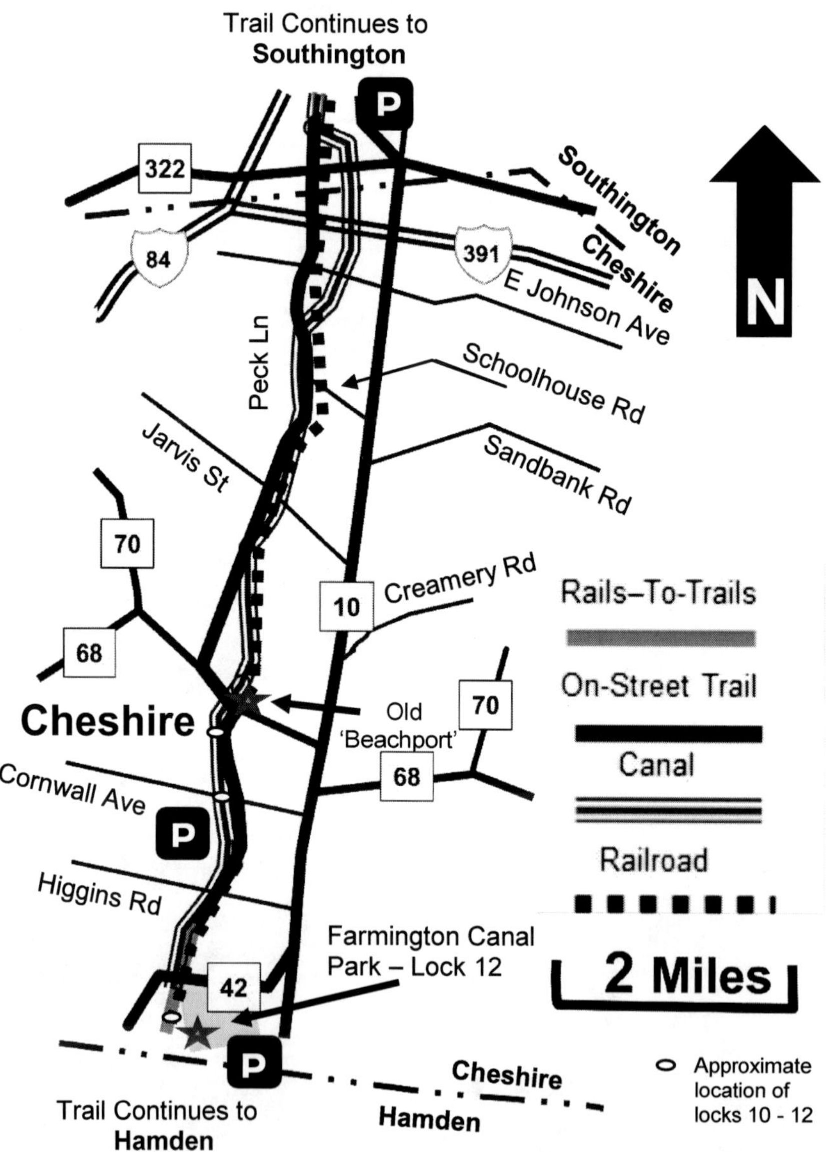

CHESHIRE FARMINGTON CANAL HERITAGE TRAIL

CHESHIRE RAIL TRAIL

Rail Trail:

⊗**TRAILHEAD:** Cheshire, CT. Park at the Farmington Canal Park. CT-42/455 North Brooksvale Rd, Cheshire, CT.

← Bike west on CT-42/N Brooksvale Rd and take a quick → right onto the Farmington Canal Heritage Trail (FCHT) traveling 1.5 mi. FCHT ends. ***NOTE: Now you are off the trail you will be traveling on-street.***

→ Turn right on Cornwell Ave and travel a few feet turning left onto Willow St, (GPS parking 480 Cornwall Ave).

← Left onto Willow St.

↑ From Willow Street travel 0.6 mi. to CT-68 W/Ct-70 W/W Main St.

← Bearing left at the junction, travel along busy CT-68 W/CT-70 W/W Main St for 0.6 mi. taking a → right onto Peck Ln.

↑ Continue north on Peck Ln. 2.0 mi. (be careful and DO NOT go right onto Sandbank Rd).

← Be careful and turn left at Sandbank Rd still on Peck Ln. traveling 1.7 mi.

↑ Continue onto Canal St where you will find the entrance to FCHT (near Canal St and CT-322/Meriden – Waterbury Turnpike).

⊗**TRAILHEAD:** Southington, CT. Near the junction of Canal St and CT-322/Meriden – Waterbury Turnpike, at the entrance to the Farmington Heritage Trail, parking is available on Canal St.

NOTE: Southington trailhead on CT-322/Meriden – Waterbury Turnpike can be reached via US-84, EXIT 28 or nearby US-691, EXIT 3 about 1 mile away by car.

DIRECTIONS SOUTH? Go to the Rail Trail Guide at the end of this chapter.

PARKING ACCESS:

Cheshire, CT

- **Trailhead GPS:** 455 North Brooksvale Rd, ZIP06410. Park at the Farmington Canal Park. CT-42/455 North Brooksvale Rd, Cheshire, CT.

- Mid trail GPS parking: 480 Cornwall Ave, Cheshire, CT.

Southington

- **Trailhead GPS:** 447 Canal St, ZIP 06489. Near the junction of Canal St and CT-322/Meriden – Waterbury Turnpike, at the entrance to the Farmington Heritage Trail, parking is available on Canal St

CHESHIRE HISTORY

Cheshire, the second town north of New Haven, is located in the historic Indian Naugatuck Valley. "Once part of Wallingford and known as North Farms, Cheshire separated from Wallingford in 1780. . ." Of interest is a book by Joseph Perkins Beach entitled "History of Cheshire, Connecticut from 1694 to 1840" (see source link). The book describes Cheshire and surrounding towns, references to King Philip's War, building fortifications, Indian trouble, powder firearms, parceling out land by lots and many other interesting period facts. Cheshire was and is a farming community. It is still a rural community with agriculture with some state run facilities.

CHESHIRE CANAL HISTORY

Where's the canal? In Cheshire, the canal and the railroad bed follows each other most of the way north as it meanders and traverses the earth contours east of the Farmington Heritage Canal Trail from border-to-border (see map).

Watercolor image of canal and draft horses in the Farmington Canal Historic Park, Cheshire's Lock 12. Watercolor by Robert R. Madison

Canal History: Charles Rufus Harte commented to the Connecticut Society of Engineers that "On November 24, 1827, water was let into the so-called Cheshire Summit level, and there was a great celebration". A port and a store, along with a loading platform, were located next to the canal. The port was near West Cheshire and it was christened 'Beachport' . . ." 'Beachport' is just north of Lock 10 where the old rail bed or the Farmington Canal Heritage Trail intersects CT-68/Cornwall Ave. Irish workers, working in the swamplands, found it very difficult and expensive to 'muck' or dig out the canal in this section.

Most of the 60 locks along the canal system are long gone. Cheshire had three locks (Locks, 10, 11 and 12). Cheshire's Lock 12 still exists and it is located next to the bicycle path in the Farmington Canal Park off North Brooksvale Road. Lock 12 survived because it was eventually made of stone (the original wood lining rotted away). In 1980, the Cheshire Parks Department and the National Park Service restored the lock. When in operation, it took about five minutes to lock through the

9′ change in height. The Lockmaster's house still exists next to the lock. And, a museum is located next to the house!

In order to cross the Ten Mile River in northern Cheshire, an 18′ culvert along with a huge curved earthen project some 1200′ long and 40′ high were constructed. The earthen canal was intentionally breached four times over the life of the canal system.

A trip from New Haven to Cheshire took about 5 hours. One year, in 1843 during the summer, a drought caused the canal to be closed from July to September, and just when navigation started again, the canal bank broke open! A man from Cheshire confessed years later on his death bed that in 1843, he purposely broke open the canal bank above Ten Mile River because he had a grudge against a man living just below the canal and he wanted to flood him out.

The Cheshire Historical Society has produced a book entitled *'REFLECTIONS ON THE CANAL IN CHESHIRE, A Scrap-Book Account'* compiled by Raimon L Beard [refer to credits in the back of this guide]. The book contains a wealth of information in the form of newspaper articles or noteworthy authors who wrote articles about the canal. For example, the author quoted from "The Canal" an address delivered by Julius Gay in 1899 [page 38] the following "The farmers hated the canal. The water leaked through the towpath and turned their meadows into swamps. The rickety bridges frightened their cattle and were set so high that is was hard to draw a good-sized load of hay over one, but it will be hard to find one who was a boy in those happy days speak evil of the Farmington Canal". In the same paragraph, Julius Gay goes on to say "I remember standing one fine autumn day on the old 'Yellow Store Basin' wharf and watch a packet-boat sail away. . ."

CHESHIRE RAIL TRAIL

Cheshire's Lock 12 Historic Park is a restored section of the Farmington Canal and includes a 3-mile hiking/biking trail, museum, Lockkeeper's house, arch, and picnic/parking.

CANAL RAILROAD

Where's the railroad? In Cheshire, the railway and the Farmington Canal are the same, boarder-to-border. Bicycling is mainly 'on street.'

Railroad History: Construction of The New Haven & Northampton RR (NH&N) began in New Haven to Hamden and the first stage ended in Cheshire in 1847. The route chosen was along the original old Farmington Canal right-of-way (and some sections of the old Cheshire Turnpike). Between 1848 and 1869 the route was operated by other railroad companies including the New Haven & Northampton RR, the New York & Northampton RR, the New Haven RR, the Penn Central RR and Boston & Maine RR and lastly CONRAIL. The railway was finally abandoned in 1987.

CHESHIRE RAIL TRAIL

Cheshire Farmington Canal Park Culvert. This culvert or arch connects the railroad bed as it passes over the lower portion of what was then the canal. Today, the rail-trail passes over the canal. The bicyclist or hiker can use the park to rest and maybe visit the museum.

BICYCLE REPAIR AND RENTAL

Cheshire Cycle & Repair
Serving the Cheshire Area
203 250-9996
http://www.cheshirecycle.com

Cheshire Cycle
3550 Whitney Ave
Hamden, CT
203 891-5320
http://www.cheshirecycle.com/

Play It Again Sports
685 Queen St, Unit 8
Southington, CT 06489
860 621-0045
www.playitagainsportssouthingtonct.com

OFF RAIL TRAIL EXCURSIONS

(Excursions may or may not require bicycles)

1. Cheshire Town Hall
84 South Main St
Cheshire, CT 06410
203 271-6630
www.cheshirect.org

2. Many shopping plazas or malls exist along this section of the trail.

3. Cheshire Public Library
104 Main St
Cheshire, CT 06410
203 272-2245
www.cheshirelibrary.org

4. Bartlem Recreation Area
(520 South Main St)

5. Cheshire Historical Society
43 Church Dr
Cheshire, CT 06410
203 272-2574
www.cheshirehistory.org

Cheshire Park
(intersection of Highland Ave and Stony Hill Rd)

Farmington Canal linear Park
(490 Cornwall Ave or 487 North Brooksvale Rd)

McNamara Legion Field
(550 Weise Rd)

Mixville Recreation Area
(1300 Notch Rd)

Quinnipiac Recreation Area
(1325 Cheshire St)

Roaring Brook Falls
(827 Roaring Brook Rd)

RAIL TRAIL GUIDE

NORTH

HEADING SOUTH

MILES N		MILES S
6.4	⊗ **TRAILHEAD @** Southington, CT, Canal Street	0
	↑ Head south on Canal St from FCHT crossing CT-322/Meriden-Waterbury Turnpike picking up Peck Ln careful to go → right at the junction of Sandbank Rd.	1.7
	↑ Continuing on Peck Ln (until turning left at the Junction of CT-68/E CT-70 E/West Main St.).	2.0
	← Left on CT-68/E CT-70 E/West Main St to take a right on Willow St.	0.6
	→ Right on Willow St to take a quick right on Cornwall Ave. at the end of Willow St.	0.6
	← On Cornwall Ave. travel a few feet turning left onto Farmington Canal Heritage Trail.	0
	← Arriving at CT-43/N Brooksvale Rd take a short left and turn right onto the Farmington Canal Heritage Trail (FCHT) and parking or go to Lock 12.	1.5
3.7	→ Right onto Peck Lane traveling north being careful to turn left onto Sandbank Rd another 1.7 miles onto Canal St and the entrance to FCHT/parking.	
0.6	→Willow St ends. Take a left from Willow St onto CT-68 W/CT-70 W/W Main St to Peck Ln.	
0.6	↑ Willow St to CT-68 W/CT-70 W/W Main St.	
0	← Cornwall Ave and travel a few feet turning left onto Willow St.	
1.5	→ Follow the FCHT to the end and turn right onto Cornwall Ave.	
0	→ Turn right onto the Farmington Canal Heritage Trail (FCHT).	
0	⊗ **TRAILHEAD @** Cheshire, CT, N Brooksvale Road	6.4

HEADING NORTH

SOUTH

NOTES

SECTION 4: SOUTHINGTON
(SOUTHINGTON RAILS TO TRAILS GREENWAY)

Common Names: East Coast Greenway, Southington Rails-to-Trails Greenway, the Farmington Canal Heritage Trail and the New Haven & Northampton Canal.

Route: Canal St, Southington to Norton Park Rd, Plainville.
Total Distance: 8.0 miles or 50 - 70 minutes.

Ride Details: Skill level is moderate and some trail routes include busy 'on street' traffic. Elevation gain is minimal.

Significant Canal Features: Southington has three locks (Locks 7, 8 and 9). Packet boats stopped at Southington's Merriam's Basin, located just west of Eightmile River near Marion Ave somewhere under US/84, to take on or unload supplies. As noted earlier, the canal meanders under US/84 and away from bicycle trails until it passes CT/177 in Plainville and can be seen in Norton Park.

Strolling along Southington's rail-trail near the Milldale train depot.

SOUTHINGTON RAIL TRAIL MAP

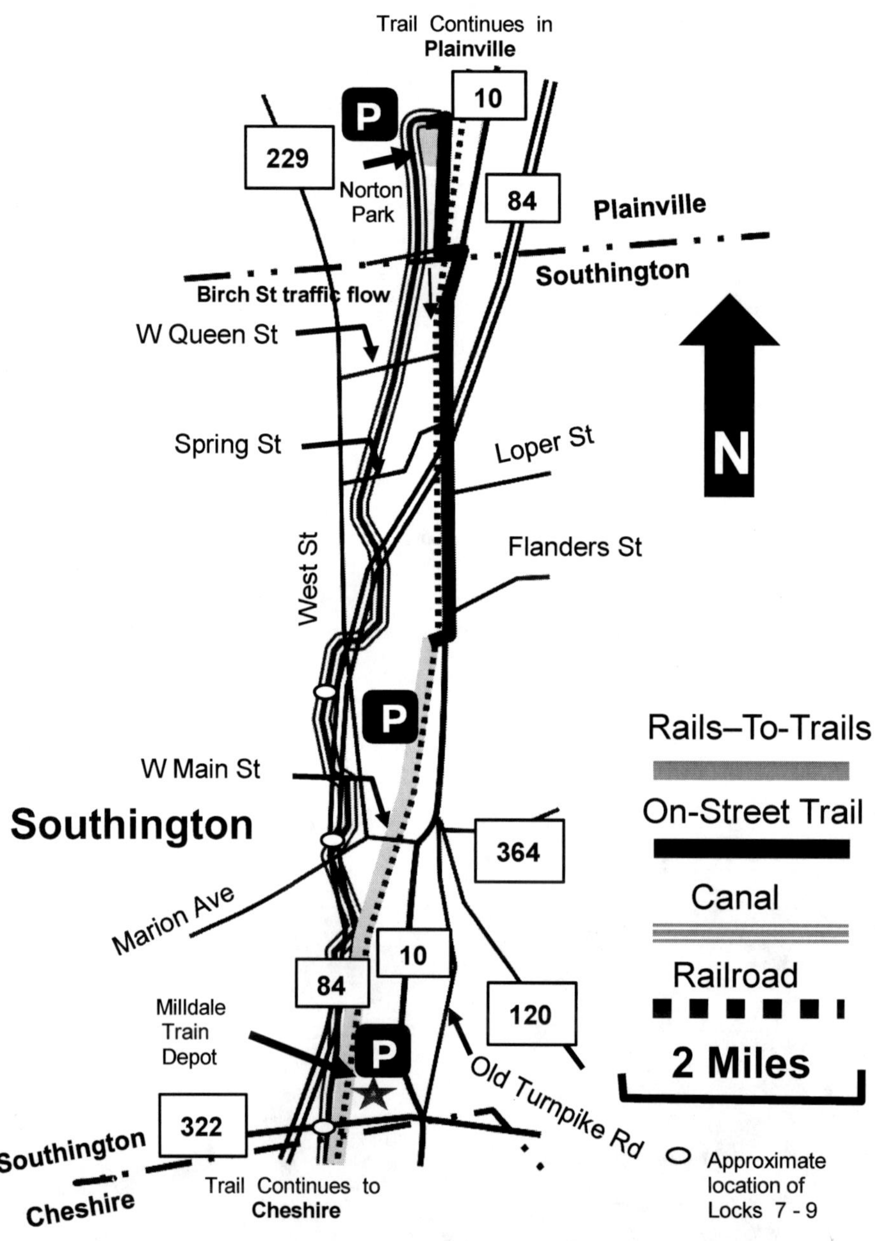

SOUTHINGTON RAILS TO TRAILS GREENWAY

SOUTHINGTON RAIL TRAIL

Rail Trail:

⊗**TRAILHEAD**: Southington, CT. Near the junction of Canal St and CT-322/Meriden – Waterbury Turnpike, at the entrance to the Farmington Heritage Trail (FCHT), parking is available on Canal St

NOTE: Southington trailhead on CT-322/Meriden – Waterbury Turnpike can be reached via US-84, EXIT 28 or nearby US-691, EXIT 3 about 1 mile away by car.

↑ At the FCHT entrance, travel north 3.9 mi. arriving at Hart St (Kane Street junction).

The FCHT ends here! Unless construction enhances the rail trail one must use 'on-street' hiking or biking.

> *NOTICE: Until Southington's Rails-to-Trails Greenway is complete, bikers must make a decision to follow the heavily trafficked CT-10/North Main Street route to Plainville.*

→ Turn right and bike a short distance on Hart St to Curtiss St (FCHT ends) traveling 0.2 mi to North Main St.

← Take a left onto CT-10 N/North Main St (switching to Queens St and under CT-84) for 2.7 mi.

← Take a left onto Town Line Rd/CT-177 0.2 mi. (NOTE: Birch Rd 0.5 mi. before Town Line Rd is one way southbound for vehicles).

→ Turn right onto CT-177 South Washington St going 0.8 mi.

← Turn left onto Norton Park Rd traveling about 0.1 mi. entering Norton Park.

⊗**TRAILHEAD:** Plainville, CT. Parking at Norton Park off Norton Park Rd. Use Norton Park as your base for excursions along the rail-trail (north or south). Restored canal and various monuments are located in Norton Park.

DIRECTIONS SOUTH? Go to the Rail Trail Guide at the end of this chapter.

PARKING ACCESS:

Southington

•**Trailhead GPS:** 447 Canal St, ZIP 06489. Near the junction of Canal St and CT-322/Meriden – Waterbury Turnpike, at the entrance to the Southington Rails-to-Trails Greenway or FCHT entrance. Parking is available on Canal St

•Parking at the intersection of CT-322/Meriden – Waterbury Turnpike and Canal St shopping near the Southington Rails-to-Trails Greenway or FHT entrance.

•Parking mid-trail on FCHT @ 50 Mill St, Southington, CT.

Plainville, CT

•**Trailhead GPS:** 100 Norton Park, ZIP 06062. Just off Norton Park Rd in Plainville.

•Park and visit at the Plainville Historic Society on 29 Pierce St

•Parking at the Paderewski Park off Cleveland Memorial /College St

SOUTHINGTON HISTORY

Southington was originally part of Farmington and known originally as "South Farmington" and the name shortened along the way to Southington. The town separated from Farmington in 1779. "Southington became a thriving community with the construction of dwellings, taverns, and stores. Industry flourished rapidly. In 1767, Atwater's grist mill was established and by 1790, Southington had a button factory, saw mills, a brass foundry, and potash works." According to the town's website, "Southington today is a growing community, once described as 'A Microcosm of America.' The town is located in Hartford County, within 20 miles of Hartford . ." and includes the villages of Marion, Milldale and Plantsville.

SOUTHINGTON CANAL HISTORY

Where's the canal? For the most of the distance in Southington, the canal stays west of the Southington Rails-To-Trails Greenway from the border of Cheshire about two-thirds of the way north meandering along US-84 following the earth's contours to the Plainville border (see map).

Canal History: Earlier canal locks were constructed with dry masonry walls with a timber lining against the earth. A practice that resulted in wood that decayed rapidly. "...the later built locks . . . , in both states, were of masonry laid in 'hydraulic' cement, the discovery that there was suitable raw material in quantity at Southington". Southington has three locks (Locks 7, 8 and 9). Packet boats stopped at Southington's Merriam's Basin, located just west of Eightmile River near Marion Ave somewhere under US/84, to take on or unload supplies. North of Merriam's Basin and Lock 7, waste weirs were built to dispose of excess water (to prevent water from over spilling the canal).

Of interest is that the distance between Southington's Lock 7 and the next Lock located in East Granby is about 26 miles (the 'Long Level' passed through Southington, Plainville, Farmington, Avon, Simsbury and East Granby). In Granby, six locks brought the water level high enough to match the water level of Congamond Lake in Southwick, Massachusetts (220' above sea level). As time progressed, the canal was extended all the way to the Connecticut River. A canal boat called Enterprise was the first boat that traveled through Southington. The canal was not an overall success; however, the canal did experience some successful years. In the early 1840's, before the canal was ultimately closed because of the railroad.

Another interesting comment by canal enthusiast Charles Harte was regarding the first usage of propeller driven canal boats (Beecher Screw Propeller or Ericsson Propeller) "between West Cheshire – Beachport in those days – and Milldale" now Southington. When propeller driven vessels were used by vessels in the canal they tended to upset the canal's walls.

SOUTHINGTON RAIL TRAIL

Packet boat horses could pull a boat about 4 miles per hour and were changed every 10 miles. The towpaths that the animals traveled on were at least 10 feet wide. Heading north, Lock 7 in Southington was the beginning of the 'Long Level', a level area some 26 miles long without locks

Packet boats stopped at Southington's Merriam's Basin located just west of Eightmile River near Marion Ave to take on or unload supplies. Watercolor by Robert R. Madison

Part of the 'Long Level' as the canal passes through Southington.

Where's the railroad? The rail tracks and the Southington Rails-To-Trails Greenway are one and the same.

Railroad History: Southington work on the New Haven & Northampton RR (NH&N) Canal Railroad was during the 1846-48 timeframe (the next town up, Plainville, started work during 1846 and the section from Plainville to Farmington and Avon opened in 1850). The Southington Milldale Train Depot, located on 447 Canal Street, was built in 1890 and is open to the public, but check on availability before visiting.

Construction continued north so that ultimately the rail line to Westfield and Northampton was finished by 1856. Between 1856 and 1991 when the rail line was finally abandoned, the route was operated one way or the other by the New Haven & Northampton RR, the New York, New Haven & Hartford RR, the New Haven RR, the Penn Central RR and Boston & Maine RR and lastly CONRAIL.

Milldale railroad depot along Southington's rail-trail.

BICYCLE REPAIR AND RENTAL

Play It Again Sports
685 Queen St, Unit 8
Southington, CT 06489
860 621-0045
www.playitagainsportssouthingtonct.com

Renaissance Cyclery
49 W Main St
Plainville, CT 06062
860 747-2909

OFF RAIL TRAIL EXCURSIONS

(Excursions may or may not require bicycles)

1.Southington Town Hall
75 Main St
Southington, CT 06489
860 276-6211
www.southington.org

2. Norton Park in Plainville, CT
is a good stopping point or rest area for walkers and bicyclists.

3. The Southington or Milldale Train Depot
447 Canal St, adjacent to the Southington Rails-to-Trails Greenway.

4. Barnes Museum
85 North Main St
Southington, CT 06489
860 628-5426
www.barnesmuseum.wordpress.com

5. Mount Southington
396 Mt Vernon Rd
Plantsville, CT 06479.
(Mailing address: PO Box 347, Southington CT)
860 628-0954
www.mountsouthington.com

6. Southington Historical Society
2239 Main St
Southington, CT 06489
860 621-4811
www.southingtonhistory.org

Crescent Lake
(Shuttle Meadow, Rd)

Southington Town Green
(75 Main St)

Panthorn Park
(485 Burritt St, Plantsville)

Southington Recreation Park
(493 South End Rd, Plantsville)

Veterans Memorial Park
(776 Woodruff St, Southington)

Southington Library & Museum
(255 Main St)

RAIL TRAIL GUIDE

MILES N	NORTH	HEADING SOUTH MILES S
8.0	⊗ **TRAILHEAD @** Plainville, Norton Park Road	0
	→ Leaving Norton Park turn right onto CT-177/South Washington St.	0.1
	→ Turn right onto CT-177/South Washington St traveling to Town Line Rd.	0.8
	↑ Continue straight past Town Line Rd onto Birch Rd. [one way] to CT-10/North Main St.	0.4
	→ Right onto CT-10/Queen St switching to North Main St.	2.4
	→ Right onto Curtis St.	0.2
	← On Curtiss St, turn left onto the FCHT	0
	↑ Farmington Canal Heritage Trail to Canal St and parking.	3.9
0.1	← Turn left onto Norton Park Rd and Norton Park	
0.8	→ Right onto CT-177 South Washington St.	
0.2	← Left onto Town Line Rd/CT-177.	
2.8	← Left onto CT-10/North Main St (switching to Queen St and under CT-84) arriving at Town Line Rd.	
0.2	↑ Curtis St to North Main St.	
0	→ Right turn at Hart St and ride a short distance to Curtiss St.	
3.9	↑ FCHT entrance, travel north to Hart St. (Kane St junction).	
0	⊗ **TRAILHEAD @** Southington, CT, Canal Street	7.8
HEADING NORTH	SOUTH	

NOTES

SECTION 5: PLAINVILLE
(PLAINVILLE BICYCLE TRAVELWAY)

Common Names: East Coast Greenway, Plainville Bicycle Travelway, Farmington Canal Heritage Trail and Farmington River Trail.

Route: Norton Park Rd, Plainville to Cleveland Memorial Dr., Plainville. Total Distance: 2.5 miles or 10 to 20 minutes.

Ride Details: Skill level is easy. Elevation gain is minimal. Directions take the traveler on busy streets.

Significant Canal Features: Plainville did not have any locks; however, stopping at Norton Park, you will see an excellent example of a restored canal in Norton Park. Plainville had two basins (Whiting's Basin on the corner of US10/CT 372 and downtown Bristol Basin, a clock shipping depot) as well as a dry dock located near Bristol Basin near North Main Street and several bridges over the canal. Bridges along the canal were for the most part, rickety and poorly built.

At this West Main Street intersection in Plainville, all the methods of travel intersect; that is, the original downtown roadway, the historic canal, the railroad and today the Plainville Bicycle Travelway.

PLAINVILLE RAIL TRAIL MAP

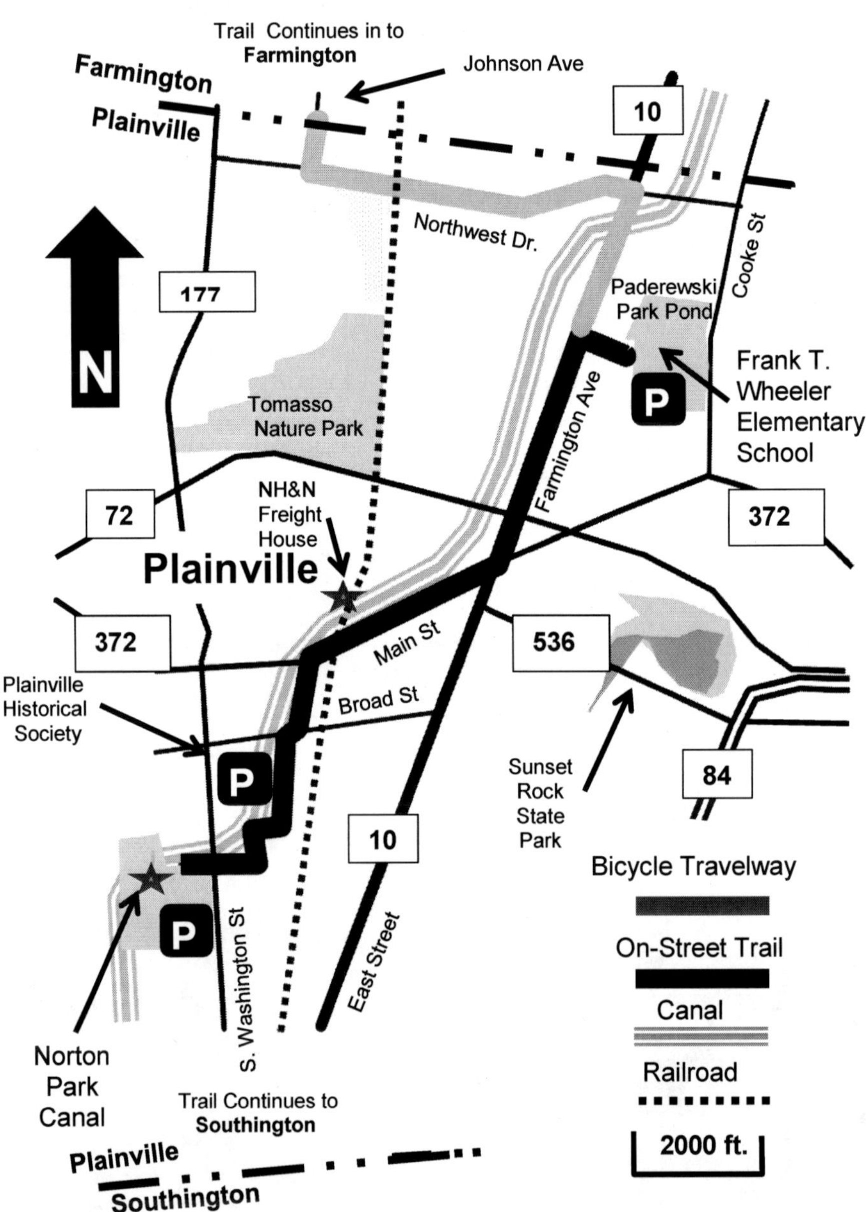

PLAINVILLE BICYCLE TRAVELWAY

PLAINVILLE RAIL TRAIL

Rail Trail:

⊗**TRAILHEAD**: Plainville, CT. Park at Norton Park. From Norton Park to Norton Park Rd (NOTE: When bicycling to Southington or Farmington, Norton Park is a good trail head to park your car), head to CT-177/S Washington St.

NOTICE: Until Plainville's Bicycle Travelway is complete, bikers must make a decision to follow the heavily trafficked CT-177/Washington Street/CT-10/Farmington route to Farmington.

← Turn left onto CT-177/S Washington St going about 0.5 mi. to Broad St

→ Right onto Broad St to Pierce St is another 0.4 mi. *(NOTE: Stop at the Plainville Historic Society on 29 Pierce St and visit the 'Ruth S. Hummel Canal Room' where many historical canal memorabilia are on display).*

→ At the end of Pierce St 0.2 mi., turn right to West Main St.

→ Right onto CT-372/West Main St for 0.6 mi. through the center of town turning left unto CT-10/Farmington Ave.

← Turn left on CT-10/Farmington Ave.

← After reaching CT-10/Farmington Ave turn right after traveling 0.8 mi. to Cleveland Memorial Dr. and Wheeler Elementary School.

The Plainville Bicycle Travelway begins at the Wheeler Elementary School near Paderewski Park (Travelway is not a rail-trail at this point in time.).

NOTE: The author chose Wheeler Elementary School location for its convenient 'town line' location to park. The author also highly recommends parking at Norton Park off Norton Park Rd and using Norton Park as your base for excursions along the bike trail both traveling north or south.

⊗TRAILHEAD: Farmington/Plainville, CT. Still in Plainville, park on-street or at 15 Cleveland Memorial Dr., 93 Cooke St, Paderewski Park off Cleveland Memorial /College St.

DIRECTIONS SOUTH? Go to the Rail Trail Guide at the end of this chapter.

PARKING ACCESS:

Plainville, CT

- •Trailhead GPS: 100 Norton Park Rd, ZIP 06062. Parking at Norton Park just off 100 Norton Park Rd in Plainville.

- •Park and visit at the Plainville Historic Society on 29 Pierce St.

- •Parking at 93 Cooke St Paderewski Park off Cleveland Memorial /College St

Farmington/Plainville, CT

- •Trailhead GPS: 15 Cleveland Memorial Dr, ZIP 06062. Park on-street or at the Frank T. Wheeler Elementary School, 15 Cleveland Memorial Dr. in Plainville.

- •Mid-trail parking: Farmington River Aqueduct Historical Site on the other side of the intersection of Aqueduct Ln. and CT10/Waterville Rd Your can reach this historic site from I-84 by taking exit 39, merging on CT-508 onto CT-4/Farmington Ave turning right 2.0 mi. onto CT-10 for another 2.0 mi. to the aqueduct.

PLAINVILLE HISTORY

The "Great Plain" is a flatland that was first settled in 1657. Originally part of Farmington, Plainville was incorporated as a separate town in 1869. According to the Town of Plainville's website, "the industrial history of Plainville dates back to about 1828 following the opening of the Farmington Canal and the early industrial sites located in what is now the business section" made up of factories, warehouses and taverns The town is located between mountain ranges: Metacomet Ridge's Bradley Mountain and Pinnacle Rock.

PLAINVILLE CANAL HISTORY

Where's the canal? The canal follows the contours of the earth west of the on-street Plainville Bicycle Travelway through Norton Park traveling north and crossing downtown Main St heading again north running west and parallel to on-street CT-10/Farmington Ave (see map).

Canal History: If the enthusiast wants to get into the details of the canal in Plainville, the author recommends an excellent work by Ruth S. Hummel entitled 'The Farmington Canal in Plainville Connecticut'. This book and other works can be purchased at the Plainville Historical Society's canal museum on 29 Pierce Street. Mrs. Hummel commented that building the canal in Plainville was somewhat easy "because of the lack of rock ledges across the Great Plain." Locks were not needed in Plainville; however, two loading basins and a dry dock for building and repairing boats were located in town. Canal history buffs will also note that the Great Plain or 'Long Level' was 26 miles in length from Southington to Granby. While in Norton Park, stop and read the 'The Farmington Canal' plaque.

Charles Rufus Harte, the noted canal historian, reported to the Connecticut Society of Engineers, that 1843 was one of the most profitable canal years. In 1843, the canal was opened to canal boats in early spring and canal travel lasted until "November 8, when occurred one of the worst of the many disastrous floods to which it had been subjected. In two days there were 30 different breaks," along the length of the canal. Mr. Harte also reported that 1844 was also a profitable year. "The canal was in operation the entire season without loss of a single day". Washouts continued to plague the canal and at the same time surveys were being conducted to determine the feasibility of constructing a railroad on the canal route. Where possible, the banks or towpaths would be used as the railroad bed. In 1846 work started on the railroad and work continued until the canal was no longer a transportation option in 1847.

PLAINVILLE RAIL TRAIL

In this painting, a canal boat and driver are being pulled by two horses with a man leading the horses as they travel north. Passengers had little room below so they would sit or stand on the flat roofs of packet boats. Meals might be served aboard or passengers brought their own food or ate at local taverns. Sleeping accommodations were flat panels that could be folded up during the day. This part of the canal is located in what is now Norton Park in Plainville. Watercolor by Robert R. Madison.

Raymond Holden watercolor painting – Canton Historical Society: This picture is hanging in the Ruth S. Hummel Canal Room at the Plainville Historical Society Museum. In a chapter on cargo in Ruth's book entitled 'The Farmington Canal in Plainville Connecticut' she talks about the importance of cargo passing through the "Bristol Basin" in Plainville.

CANAL RAILROAD

Where's the railroad? In Plainville, the railroad tracks are east of the on-street Plainville Bicycle Travelway with the tracks crossing downtown Main St heading north. The on-street bike trail stays east of the railroad tracks and is not part of the rail-trail system until past Farmington and past Avon center (see map). Railroad freight houses once existed at the end of Neal Court off East Main Street.

Railroad History: Construction of The New Haven & Northampton RR (NH&N) began in Plainville during 1846 and the section from Plainville to Farmington and Avon opened in 1850. Construction continued north so that ultimately the rail line to Westfield and Northampton was finished by 1856. Between 1856 and 1991 when the rail line was finally abandoned, the route was operated one way or the other by the New Haven & Northampton RR, the New York & Northampton RR, the New Haven RR, the Penn Central RR and Boston & Maine RR and lastly CONRAIL.

Late 1800's 'ghost' steam locomotive superimposed on a recent photograph by the author (the train is about to cross the railroad tracks on Broad Street in Plainville).

BICYCLE REPAIR AND RENTAL:

Renaissance Cyclery
49 W Main St
Plainville, CT 06062
860 747-2909

Central Wheel
62 Farmington Ave
Farmington, CT 06032
860 677-7010
www.centralwheel.com

Sports Authority
1600 S East Rd
Farmington, CT 06032
860 676-8918
www.sportsauthority.com/home

OFF RAIL TRAIL EXCURSIONS

(Excursions may or may not require bicycles)

1. Plainville Town Hall
1 Central Square
Plainville, CT 06062
860 793-0221
www.plainvillect.com

2. Shopping plazas or malls exist along this section of the trail.

3. Tomasso Nature Park
(Granger Lane off CT-177/Unionville Ave)

4. Plainville Historical Center
29 Pierce St
Plainville, CT. 06062
860 747-6577 www.plainvillehistory.org

Norton Park
(197 South Washington St)

Paderewski Park
(93 Cooke St)

Pinnacle Rock
(Metacomet Rd @ Metacomet Ridge)

Plainville Public Library
(56 East Main St)

RAIL TRAIL GUIDE

NORTH

MILES N		HEADING SOUTH MILES S
2.5		0
	⊗ **TRAILHEAD @** Plainville, CT., Cleveland Memorial Drive.	0
	← Left on CT-10/Farmington Ave to CT-32/W Main St.	0.8
	→ At CT-32/W Main St take a right and continue to Pierce St.	0.6
	← Left on Pierce St to Broad St.	0.2
	→ Right onto Broad St continue to CT-177/S Washington St and bear left toward Norton Park Rd.	0.4
	→ On CT-177/S Washinton St bear right onto Norton Park Rd to arrive at Norton Park entrance.	0.5
	→ Right onto Cleveland Memorial Dr.	
	← Left onto Cleveland Memorial Dr.	
0.8	↑ On CT-10/Farmington Ave continue to Cleveland Memorial Dr.	
0.6	← End of Pierce St take a left onto CT-32/W Main St to CT-10/Farmington Ave.	
0.2	→ Pierce St to a right onto CT-32/W Maine St.	
0.4	→ Right on Broad St to Pierce St.	
0.5	↑ From Norton Park Rd on CT-177 travel north to right on Broad St	
0	← Norton Park Rd to left onto CT-177/South Washington St.	
0	⊗ **TRAILHEAD @** Plainville, CT., Norton Park Road.	2.5
HEADING NORTH		

SOUTH

NOTES

SECTION 6: FARMINGTON
(FARMINGTON CANAL HERITAGE TRAIL)

Common Names: East Coast Greenway, Farmington Canal Heritage Trail and Farmington River Trail.

Routes: Plainville Cleveland Memorial Dr. just south of Avon still in Farmington (or, via Farmington River Aqueduct).

NOTE: The two routes outlined below allow the biker to visit the Farmington River Aqueduct Historical Site or follow the Farmington Canal Heritage Trail. See Rail Trail descriptions outlined below.

Total Distance: 5.9 miles or 30 to 40 minutes on the FCHT.

Ride Details: Farmington Canal Heritage Trail toward Avon: Skill level is easy to moderate. Elevation gain is minimal. Some parts of the route are on-street and not on the FCHT.

'On Street' Canal Route toward Avon: If taking the Farmington River Aqueduct Historic Site route, the ride skill level is moderate and a little hilly with busy on-street travel along the route. Care should be taken.

Significant Canal Features: The Farmington River Aqueduct Historical Site located at the intersection of Waterville Rd/US10 and Aqueduct Ln is an excellent stopping site if you are interested in canal history (see Canal Route to Avon below). Farmington does not have any canal locks because of the 'Long Level' between Southington and Granby; however, three basins for docking canal barges existed along with a few waste weirs that dumped excess water from the canal during periods of high rain.

Bicyclists on the Farmington Canal Heritage Trail (FCHT) crossing over the Farmington River. Rail trail users have the option of staying on the trail or going "on Street' to visit the Farmington River Aqueduct Historic Site and Fishers Meadows Recreational Area.

FARMINGTON RAIL TRAIL MAP

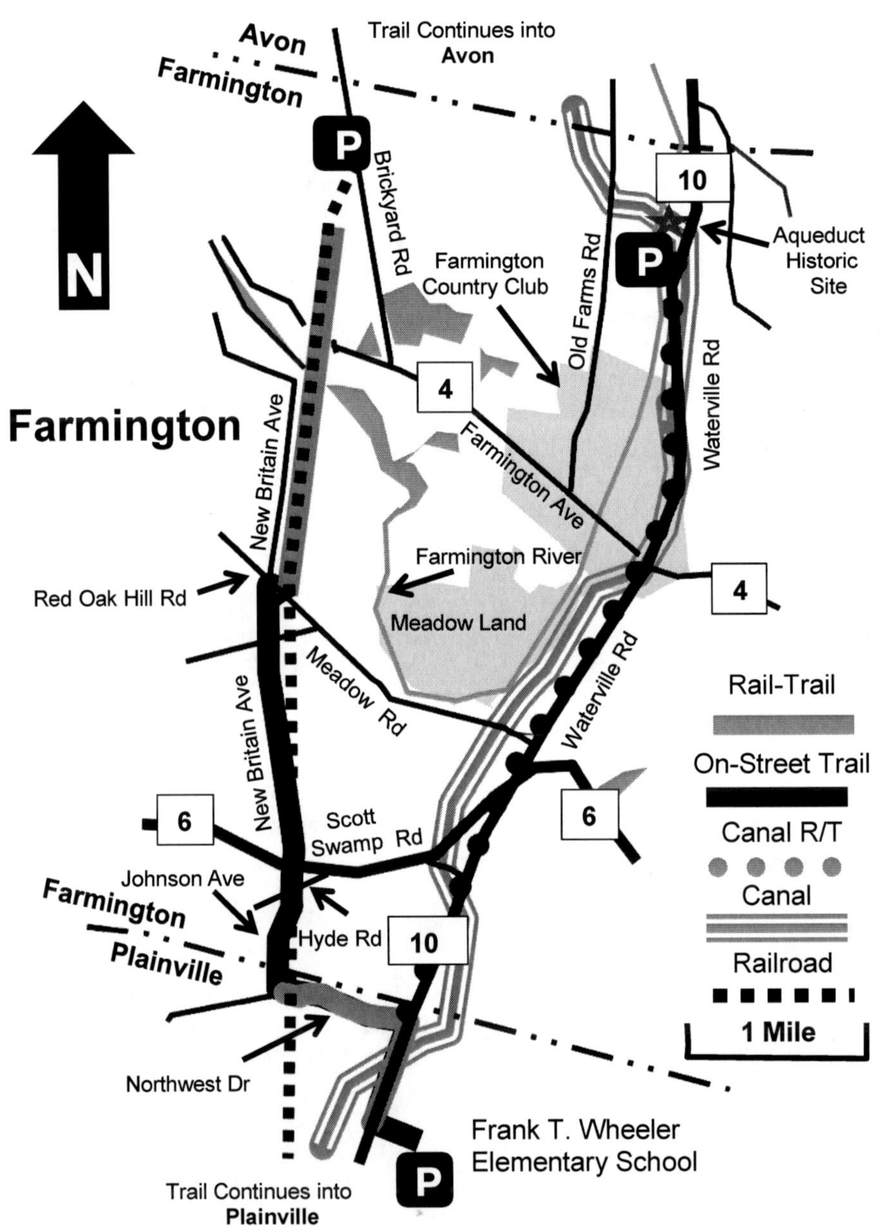

FARMINGTON CANAL HERITAGE TRAIL AND CANAL ROUTE

FARMINGTON RAIL TRAIL

RAIL TRAIL:

FCHT Route toward Avon:
5.9 miles or 30 – 40 minutes

⊗**TRAILHEAD: Plainville, CT.** Park on-street or at the Frank T. Wheeler Elementary School, 15 Cleveland Memorial Dr in Plainville.

→ Right from Cleveland Memorial/N CT-10 Farmington Ave following Farmington Ave north 0.6 mi.

← Left onto Northwest Dr and onto Plainville Bicycle Travelway 0.8 mi.

→ Right onto Johnson Ave (leaving Plainville Bicycle Travelway which heads toward Unionville Ave) 0.3 mi.

→ Right onto Hyde Rd 0.2 mi.

← Left onto New Britain Ave 2.0 mi.

→ Slight right on Red Oak Rd to pick up the FCHT on your left.

← Left on the FCHT 1.9 mi.

→ Right onto Brickyard Rd 0.1 mi.

⊗**TRAILHEAD: Farmington, CT.** FCHT parking at 225 Brickyard Rd.

RAIL TRAIL:

Canal Route toward Avon:
5.5 miles or 30 – 45 minutes

⊗**TRAILHEAD: Plainville, CT.** Park on-street or at the Frank T. Wheeler Elementary School, 15 Cleveland Memorial Dr in Plainville.

→ Right from Cleveland Memorial/CT-10 Farmington Ave continuing onto Main St with Farmington Country Club on your left onto Waterville Rd then onto Aqueduct Ln on your left. 5.5 mi.

NOTE: The Farmington River Aqueduct Historical Site is about 2.0 mi. north of the Farmington Country Club and on the opposite side of Aqueduct Ln and CT10/Waterville Rd.

⊗**TRAILHEAD: <u>Farmington, CT.</u>** FCHT parking at the Farmington River Aqueduct Historical Site on CT-10/275 Waterville Rd in Farmington, ZIP 06032.

DIRECTIONS SOUTH? Go to the Rail Trail Guide at the end of this chapter.

PARKING ACCESS:

<u>Plainville/Farmington, CT</u>

- Trailhead GPS: 15 Cleveland Memorial Dr ZIP 06062. Park on-street or at the Frank T. Wheeler Elementary School, 15 Cleveland Memorial Dr in Plainville.

- Parking on the Farmington River Aqueduct Historical Site located on the other side of the intersection of Aqueduct Ln and CT10/Waterville Rd. You can reach this historic site from I-84 by taking exit 39, merging on CT-508 onto CT-4/Farmington Ave turning right 2.0 mi. onto CT-10 for another 2.0 mi. to the aqueduct.

- Reach the Conklin Nature Trail parking lot after driving a short distance down Meadow Rd. Two other parking lots are close to the Farmington Canal Heritage Trail.

- Parking GPS: Fishers Meadows Trailhead: 304 Old Farms Rd, Farmington, CT along canal route toward Avon.

- Parking near FCHT/Tunxis Meade Park, Farmington, CT.

- Parking on 996 New Britain Ave, Farmington, CT.

<u>Farmington/Avon, CT</u>

- Trailhead GPS: FCHT parking at 225 Brickyard Rd, ZIP 06032. FCHT parking at 225 Brickyard Rd, Farmington, CT.

• Trailhead GPS: Canal Route parking at the Farmington River Aqueduct Historical Site, CT-10/275 Waterville Rd, Farmington, ZIP 06032.

• Trailhead GPS: 1 Fisher Rd, Avon, CT. FCHT parking at the corner of Simsbury Rd/Mountain View Ave/Fisher Rd

• Parking at various downtown Avon Center locations.

FARMINGTON HISTORY

Farmington, during its early years, was known as the "Mother of Towns" because it was ultimately divided into nine separate towns including Avon, Bristol, Plainville, New Britain, Southington and Burlington. Farmington was the largest community in the Connecticut Colony. Farmington was first settled in 1640 by residents of Hartford who wanted to settle west of the Connecticut River. As a residential suburb of the greater Hartford area, Farmington has maintained its historical character because its citizens are committed to maintaining its rural character.

FARMINGTON CANAL HISTORY

Where's the canal? The canal meanders and follows the earth contours back and forth along CT-10 ending just south of Avon. *NOTE: The rail trail route described below follows the canal trail route along CT-10/Waterville Rd to the Farmington River Aqueduct Historical Site rather than the Farmington Canal Heritage Trail (FCHT) route. If you look carefully at the contours in the Farmington Country Club, you should see some ancient canal features.* The FCHT takes the biker downtown into Farmington center (see Rail Trail Route description below).

Canal History: Farmington clearly was one the earlier communities to recognize the importance of rail trail development. The Farmington Canal Heritage Trail is recognized the world over. Back on January 29, 1822, representatives from seventeen interested villages met in Farmington to start the canal project. Their meeting place still exists at the Cowles' home on Main St They hired the Chief Engineer, Benjamin Wright, of the Erie Canal fame to develop a preliminary survey of the best route between New Haven and Northampton.

Engineer Charles R. Harte commented that "An aqueduct of 200 feet in length, consisting of stone abutments and piers supporting a wooden trunk. . . will be required across the Farmington River" but the dimensions were later raised and lengthened to 280 feet to "do away with the lock on this section".

On June 20, 1828 the first canal boat was built and then launched at 'Pitkin's Basin' and the boat was given the name James Hillhouse (Honorable James Hillhouse was an early supporter of the canal and has a street named after him in New Haven). Local merchants used the term 'Port of Farmington' to invite travelers to stop and purchase their wares. Two other basins (another name for ports) exist in Farmington: The first is where the canal crossed Farmington Ave/CT4 and the second near where the canal crosses Town Farm Rd.

"THE AQUEDUCT CONTAINED a wooden trough 280 feet long, six feet deep and 14 feet wide, supported by two huge abutments at each end and six massive sandstone piers rising 40 feet from the solid rock of the river bed. A six-foot wide wooden platform elevated along the top of the piers served as a towpath for the horses dragging the boats through the aqueduct's waterway". Quote from a plaque at the Farmington Canal Aqueduct in Farmington, CT. Watercolor by Robert R Madison

In 1836 the Farmington Canal Company and the Hampshire and Hampden Company of Massachusetts became the New Haven and Northampton Canal Company.

A 1869 photograph by Karl Klauser of the Farmington Aqueduct. The aqueduct was destroyed as a result of a flood in 1955.

Feeder lines from major water sources kept water in the canal system. The Farmington River's feeder line kept water in the system. A dam located just above Unionville diverted water from the river to the canal. The marvel was that the Farmington River was the major source of water north to Granby all the way south to New Haven!

As you use the rail trail you will see many references on plaques to organizations that supported the rail trail concept as well as the canal. Names such as the Farmington Valley Greenway; the Farmington Canal Heritage Trail; the Farmington Valley Trails Council; the Farmington Canal Rail-to-Trail Association; the Farmington Canal Greenway Vision Trail and other organizations, supporters and individuals. The author cannot begin to mention everyone who made the rail trail possible. As you use the rail trail, support the rail trail concept and help out in any way you can. . .

CANAL RAILROAD

Where's the railroad? In Farmington, the rail tracks are west of on-street Farmington Canal Heritage Rail Trail (from the junction of CT-10/ CT-4, travel west for 2 miles along CT-4 to where the tracks cross the Farmington River [just east of Farmington's Town Hall on Monteith Dr.]). The rail tracks do not converge with the FCHT until downtown Avon (see map).

Railroad History: Construction of The New Haven & Northampton RR (NH&N) began in Plainville then on to Farmington and Avon in 1850 and the section was opened in 1850. Construction continued north so that ultimately the rail line to Westfield and Northampton was finished by 1856. Between 1856 and 1991 when the rail line was finally abandoned, the route was operated one way or the other by the New Haven & Northampton RR, the New York & Northampton RR, the New Haven RR, the Penn Central RR and Boston & Maine RR and lastly CONRAIL.

Farmington Railroad Station on Depot Street.

BICYCLE REPAIR AND RENTAL

Central Wheel, 62 Farmington Ave
Farmington, CT 06032
860 677-7010
www.centralwheel.com

Sports Authority
1600 S East Rd
Farmington, CT 06032
860 676-8918
www.sportsauthority.com/home

Renaissance Cyclery
49 W Main St
Plainville, CT 06062
860 747-2909

Bicycle Cellar & Repair Shop
532 Hopmeadow St
Simsbury, CT 06070
860 658-1211
http://www.bicyclecellar.com

OFF RAIL TRAIL EXCURSIONS

(Excursions may or may not require bicycles)

1. Farmington Town Hall
1 Monteith Dr
Farmington, CT 06032
860 675-2300
www.farmington-ct.org

2. Hill-Stead Museum
(35 Mountain Rd)

3. Shopping plazas or malls are adjacent to the trail on US-10/ Hopmeadow St

4. Farmington River Aqueduct Historical Site
(Aqueduct Ln. and CT10/Waterville Rd).

5. Farmington Historical Society
138 Main St
Farmington, CT 06032
860 678-1645
www.farmingtonhistoricalsociety-ct.org

Stanley-Whitman House
(37 High St)

Farmington Memorial Forest
(Plainville Ave)

Farmington Reservoir Trail
(Reservoir Rd)

Shade Swamp Sanctuary
(CT-6/New Britain Ave)

Suburban Park
(CT-167/Cottage St)

Batterson Park
(Batterson Rd)

Farmington River Tubing
(42 Main St., New Hartford, CT)

Old Stone Schoolhouse
(93 Coppermine Rd)

Lewis Walpole Library
(154 Main St)

Farmington Library
(6 Monteith Dr)

RAIL TRAIL GUIDE

NORTH

HEADING SOUTH

MILES N		MILES S
5.9	⊗ **TRAILHEAD @** Farmington CT., Brickyard Road	0
	← On Brickyard Rd, turn left onto FCHT crossing over the Farmington River.	1.9
	→ Slight right on Red Oak Rd to New Britain Ave. on left.	0.1
	← Left onto New Britain Ave.	2.0
	→ Right on Hyde Rd.	0.2
	← Left onto Johnson Ave.	0.3
	← Left onto Plainville Bicycle Travelway.	0.4
	← Left on Northwest Dr.	0.4
	→ Right onto Farmington Ave/CT-10.	0.6
	← Left on Cleveland Memorial, Plainville, CT.	
0.1	→ Right onto Brickyard Rd.	
1.9	← Left onto the FCHT crossing over the Farminton River.	
0.0	→ Slight right on Red Oak Rd to FCHT on left.	
2.0	← Left onto New Britain Ave.	
0.2	→Right onto Hyde Rd.	
0.3	→ Right onto Johnson Ave.	
0.8	← Left onto Northwest Dr.	
0.6	→ Intersection of Cleveland Memorial /N CT-10 Farmington Ave following Farmington Ave. north.	
0	⊗ **TRAILHEAD @** Plainville, CT., Cleveland Memorial Avenue.	5.9

HEADING NORTH

SOUTH

NOTES

SECTION 7: AVON
(FARMINGTON CANAL HERITAGE TRAIL)

Common Names: East Coast Greenway and Farmington Canal Heritage Trail.

Route: Farmington Canal Heritage Trail in Farmington just south of Avon to Sperry Park in Avon. *NOTE: The two routes outlined below allow the biker to visit the Farmington River Aqueduct Historical Site or follow the Farmington Canal Heritage Trail.* See Rail Trail descriptions outlined below.

Total Distance: 4.6 miles or 25 to 40 minutes on FCHT.

Ride Details: Skill level is easy to moderate. Elevation gain is minimal.

Significant Canal Features: Avon did not have any locks slowing water traffic. Two stone markers announce the crossing of Albany Turnpike near the Avon Historical Center.

Visit the Avon Historical Society in the Library in Avon as you ride along the rail-trail. . .'on street'.

AVON RAIL TRAIL MAP

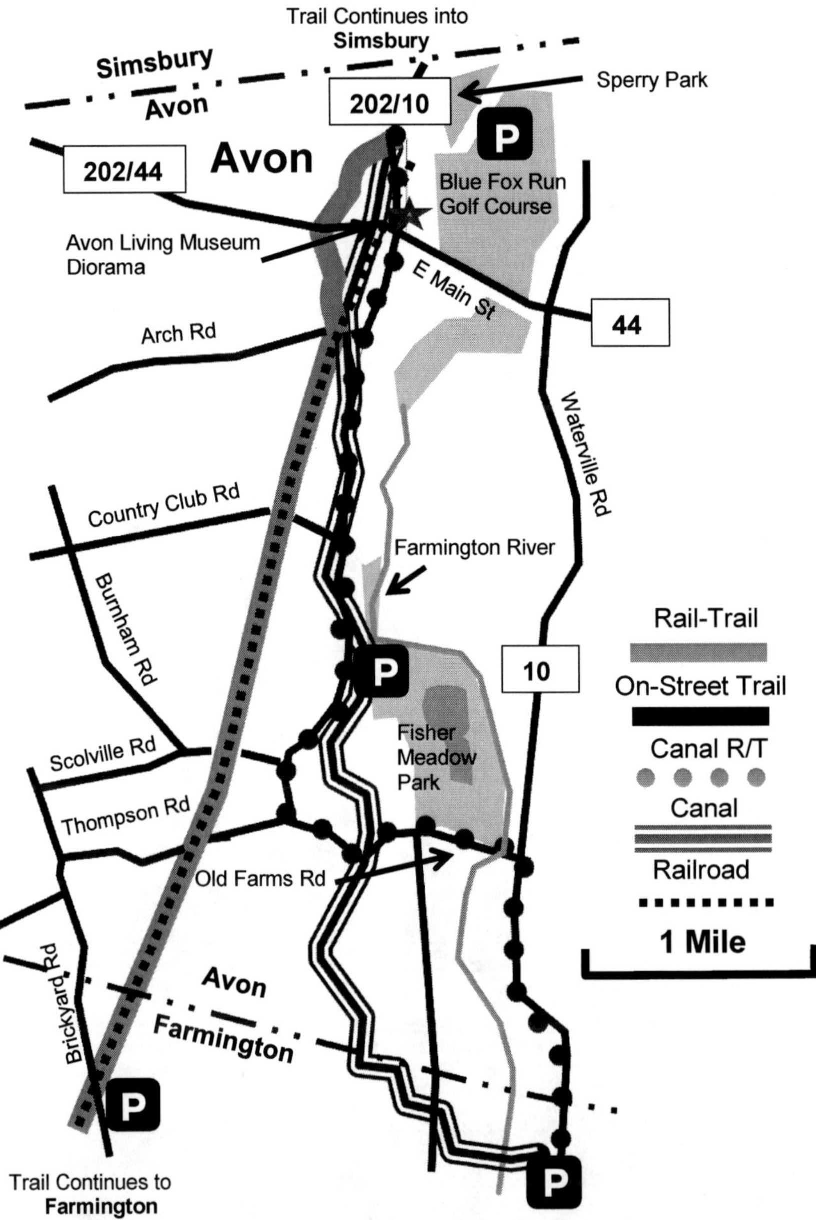

FARMINGTON CANAL HERITAGE TRAIL AND CANAL ROUTE
AVON RAIL TRAIL

RAIL TRAIL:

FCHT Route south of Avon Center:
4.9 miles or 25 – 40 minutes.

⊗**TRAILHEAD: Farmington, CT.** FCHT parking at 225 Brickyard Rd.

→ Right on Brickyard Rd to FCHT 0.1 mi.

→ Right on FCHT 3.5 mi.

→ Right onto Security Dr (from FCHT) 0.1 mi.

↑ North on Security Dr (crossing Arch Rd) 0.6 mi.

→ Right on Darling Dr (onto FCHT) and under W. Main St (CT-44/US-202) 0.2 mi. continuing onto Climax Heights Rd staying right 0.1 mi.

← Left on Ensign Dr (FCHT) 0.4 mi.

(NOTE: To visit the downtown Avon Historical Society, head up Ensign Dr a short distance and turn → right toward and onto Woodford Ave 0.2 mi. and → right onto CT-10 0.1 mi)

→ Right onto Fisher Dr (FCHT) 0.2 mi.

↑ Cross CT-10 traveling a short distance and a ← left onto the FCHT.

⊗**TRAILHEAD: Avon, CT.** FCHT parking Sperry Park or at the corner of Simsbury Rd/Mountain View Ave/Fisher Rd.

RAIL TRAIL:

Canal Route south of Avon Center:
6.1 miles or 35 – 50 minutes.

⊗**TRAILHEAD:** Farmington, CT. Parking at the Farmington River Aqueduct Historical Site is about 2.0 mi. north of the Farmington Country Club and on the opposite side of Aqueduct Ln (CT-10/Waterville Rd).

↑ North on Waterville Rd/CT-10. 1.2 mi.

← Left on Old Farms Rd 1.2 mi.

→ Left on Thompson Rd 0.4 mi.

→ Right FCHT. 2.1 mi.

→ Right on Security Dr 0.2

→ Right onto Arch Rd 0.1 mi.

← Left on Old Farms Rd 0.4 mi. until Old Farm Rd becomes CT-10/US-202/Simsbury Rd (crossing CT-44).

↑Cross CT-44 traveling a short distance and take a → right onto Enford St and a ← left onto the FCHT.

⊗**TRAILHEAD:** **Avon, CT.** FCHT parking Sperry Park or at the corner of Simsbury Rd/Mountain View Ave/Fisher Rd Since the original canal passed through downtown Avon, parking can be found at various downtown Avon Center locations before heading towards Enford St.

DIRECTIONS SOUTH? Go to the Rail Trail Guide at the end of this chapter.

PARKING ACCESS:

Farmington/Avon

- **Trailhead GPS:** FCHT parking at 225 Brickyard Rd, Farmington, CT, ZIP 06032.

- **Trailhead GPS:** Canal Route parking at the Farmington River Aqueduct Historical Site, CT-10/275 Waterville Rd, Farmington, ZIP 06032.

Avon

- **Trailhead GPS:** Parking at 70 Simsbury Rd, ZIP 06001 and also at Sperry Park along the FCHT (off Mountain View Ave).

- **Trailhead GPS:** Parking at Fishers Meadows, 800 Farms Rd, Avon, CT. ZIP 06001

- In Avon, various parking in downtown Avon Center.

AVON HISTORY

English settlers purchased land from local Indian tribes when the area was part of Farmington. The settlement was originally known as Northington or the North Parish of Farmington. Families in 1754 built their first meetinghouse at the end of Reverknolls Road. Avon ultimately was incorporated in 1830. At that time, many of Avon homes were located east of the Farmington River (along what is now Routes 202/10). Local legend suggests the name of the town came from an English river called 'Avon River'.

AVON CANAL HISTORY

Where's the canal? After the canal crosses the Farmington River just south of Avon or the Farmington River Aqueduct Historical Site, the canal meanders west of CT-10/Waterville Rd into Avon traveling east of Old Farms Rd until it crosses the intersection of CT-10/US-202/Simsbury Rd (crossing CT-44) following Simsbury Rd for a short distance.

Canal History: "The hand dug Farmington Canal, with horse drawn canal boats, ran from New Haven, CT to Northampton, MA. In Avon Center it ran north and south behind houses on the east side of Old Farms Road, crossing Albany Turnpike (currently Route 44/East Main Street) where daCapo's Restaurant stands, through the grounds of Avon Post Office and from there ran approximately along Route 10 and at times where the Rails-to-Trail is now. There was a large canal warehouse in Avon Center as well as other buildings that served this important transportation route". As noted earlier, just like in Farmington, Avon did not have any locks slowing water traffic. Two stone markers erected by the Avon Historical Society tell about the crossing of the canal over Route 44 in Avon Center. The plaque says "In 1829 the Farmington Canal opened in Avon and operated until 1847. The Markers, here and across the street, show where it crossed the Albany Turnpike now Rt. 44. They are made of the same sandstone used in the Farmington Canal construction".

AVON RAIL TRAIL

This Freight House was located near the current intersection of Route 44/East Main Street (Albany Turnpike) and Routes 202/10. Nearby were two basins where canal boats could dock or allow other canal boats to pass by easily. When this Freight House was in operation, Avon was a hub of activity because the area was located on the intersection of north/south and east/west commerce. Watercolor painting by Robert R. Madison

Canal marker outside the Avon Living Museum Diorama: "In 1829 the Farmington Canal opened in Avon and operated until 1847. The Markers, here and across the street, show where it crossed the Albany Turnpike, now Rt. 44. They are made of the same sandstone used in the Farmington Canal construction . . ."

CANAL RAILROAD

Where's the railroad? Once the old railroad bed crosses the Farmington River, it continues north well east of CT-10/US-202 and the Farmington Heritage Canal Trail until it slowly merges with Old Farm Rd just before CT-10/US-202/Simsbury Rd in Avon (crossing CT-44). Avon's railroad station was moved to a new location (15 Riverdale Farms Shopping Center, 136 Simsbury Rd) from its original location.

Abandoned railroad overpass near the corner of Old Farms Road on Arch Road.

Railroad History: Construction of The New Haven & Northampton RR (NH&N) began in Plainville to Avon in 1850. In the same time period, Avon's train depot was built by the New York & New Haven RR (the Avon Depot was moved to a shopping center on 136 Simsbury Rd. Rail construction continued north so that ultimately the rail line to Westfield and Northampton was finished by 1856. Between 1856 and 1991 when the rail line was finally abandoned, the route was operated one way or the other by the New Haven & Northampton RR, the New York & New Haven RR, the New Haven RR, the Penn Central RR and Boston & Maine RR and lastly CONRAIL.

BICYCLE REPAIR AND RENTAL FACILITIES:

Ridgeline Bikes Of Avon
175 W Main St
Avon, CT 06001
860 676-8800

Bicycle Cellar & Repair Shop
532 Hopmeadow St
Simsbury, CT 06070
860 658-1211
http://www.bicyclecellar.com

OFF RAIL TRAIL EXCURSIONS

(Excursions may or may not require bicycles)

1. Avon Town Hall
60 West Main St
Avon, CT 06001
860 409-4300
www.town.avon.ct.us

2. Avon Historical Society, Avon Living Museum Diorama
P.O. Box 448
Avon, CT 06001
860 678-7621
www.avonhistoricalsociety.org

Shopping plazas or malls are adjacent to the trail in downtown Avon.

Heublein Tower overlooking Avon.

The Avon Historical Society operates the restored Pine Grove Schoolhouse, the Avon Living Museum, and the Derrin House, a circa 1810 farmhouse.

Countryside Park
(335 Huckleberry Hill Rd)

Aslop Meadows
(US-44/Waterville Rd)

Fisher Meadows
(800 Old Farms Rd)

Found Land
(Lofgren Rd)

Hazen Park
(Nod Rd)

Huckleberry Hill Recreation Area
(116 Huckleberry Rd)
Sperry Park
(US-10/Mountain View Ave)

Sycamore Hills Recreation Area
(635 West Avon Rd)

3. The Derrin House
(249 West Avon Rd)

The Living Museum
(8 East Main St)

Pine Grove Schoolhouse
(Corner of Harris & Avon Rd)

Avon Free Library
(281 Country Club Rd)

RAIL TRAIL GUIDE

NORTH

MILES N		HEADING SOUTH MILES S
4.9	⊗ **TRAILHEAD @** Avon, Sperry Park.	0
	↑ Head toward intersection from Sperry Park/FCHT crossing CT-10 to Fisher Dr.	0.0
	↑ Continue on Fisher Dr/FCHT to left on Ensigh Dr.	0.2
	← Left onto Ensign Dr.	0.4
	→ Right onto Climax Heights Rd then slight left.	0.1
	↑ Continuing on FCHT under highway onto Darling Dr/FCHT.	0.1
	← Left onto Security Dr crossing Arch Rd.	0.6
	← Left from Security Dr then right onto FCHT to Brickyard Rd.	3.5
0.0	↑ Continue across CT-10 onto FCHT to Sperry Park.	
0.2	→ Right onto Fisher Dr.	
0.4	← Left on Ensign Dr.	
0.1	→ Right onto Darling Dr contnuing on FCHT and under highway onto Climax Heights Rd.	
0.6	↑ North on Security Dr.	
0.1	→ Right onto Security Dr (from FCHT).	
3.5	→ Right onto FCHT.	
0.0	→ On Brickyard Rd, turn right onto FCHT.	
0	⊗**TRAILHEAD @** Farmington, Brickyard Road.	4.9
HEADING NORTH		

SOUTH

SECTION 8: SIMSBURY
(FARMINGTON CANAL)

Common Names: East Coast Greenway, Farmington Canal, the Farmington Valley Greenway, the Farmington Canal Heritage Trail and the Farmington River Trail.

Route: Avon Simsbury Rd to Simsbury Tariffville Rd (Curtiss Park).
Total Distance: 6.5 miles, 40 – 60 minutes.

Ride Details: Skill level is easy to moderate. Elevation gain is minimal except near Granbrook Park Rd.

Significant Canal Features: Simsbury did not have canal locks because of the 'Long Level' between Southington and Granby; however, several culverts (Calves Tongue Brook Culvert, Hop Brook Culvert, Owens Brook Culvert, Bissell Brook Culvert, Saxon Brook Culvert) existed to carry traffic over brooks. A preserved section of the canal can be found on Old Canal Way (follow the road in) across from 200 Hopmeadow St.

Bicyclists must stop and look both ways before crossing roads.

SIMSBURY RAIL TRAIL MAP

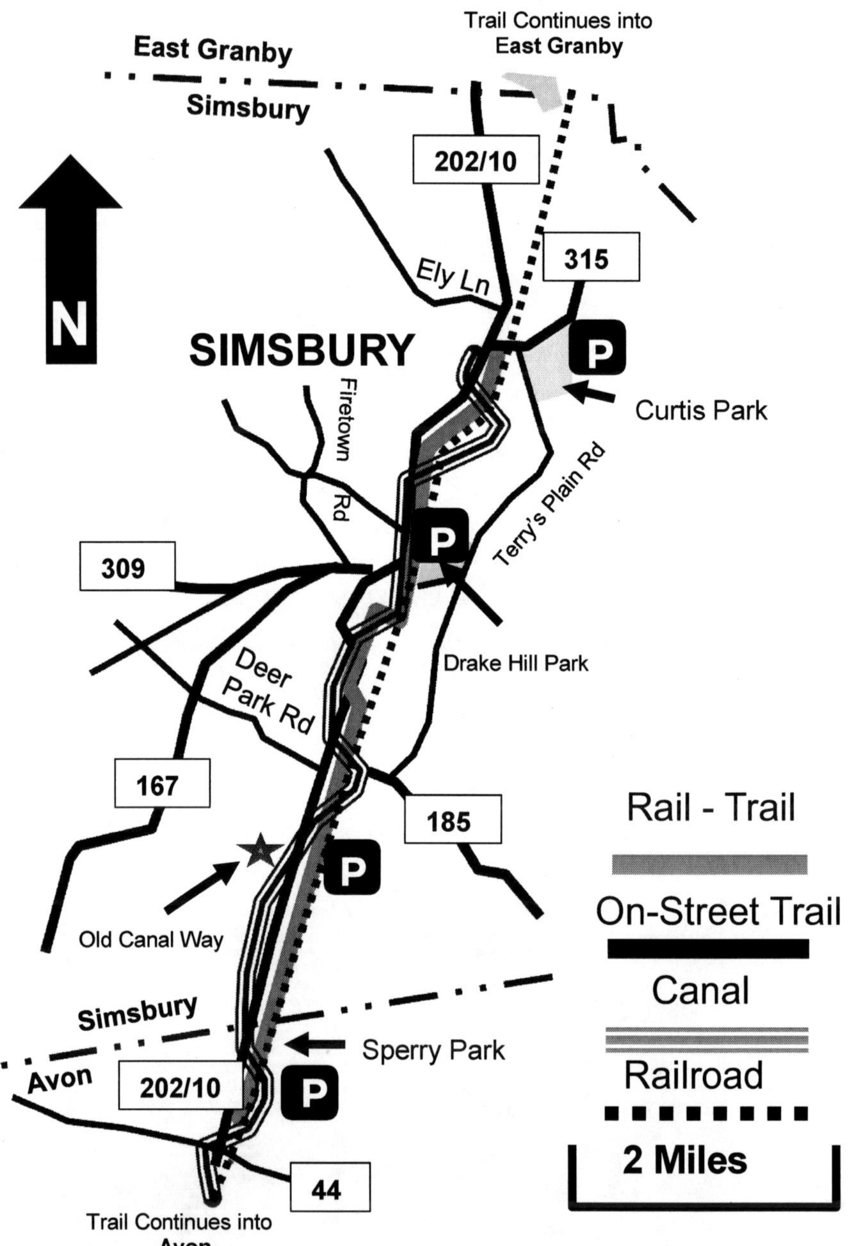

FARMINGTON CANAL HERITAGE TRAIL AND CANAL ROUTE

SIMSBURY RAIL TRAIL

RAIL TRAIL:

⊗**TRAILHEAD:** **Avon, CT.** FCHT parking at Sperry Park or FCHT at the corner of Simsbury Rd/Mountain View Ave/Fisher Rd (CT-10/US-202).

↑ From the corner of Simsbury Rd/Mountain View Ave/Fisher Rd or Sperry Park, enter FCHT. 0.1 mi.

↑ On FCHT, meeting Hopmeadow St/CT-10/US-202. 2.4 mi.

↑ On Hopmeadow St/CT-10/US-202 crossing past Winslow Pl. back onto FCHT 0.1 mi.

→ Right onto FCHT 1.7 mi.

← Left on Drake Hill Rd still on FCHT 0.1 mi

→ Right on FCHT crossing Tariffville Rd and a quick right back onto FCHT. 2.1 mi.

←FCHT parking on your left (intersection of Ely Ln/Hopmeadow St). 0.1 mi.

⊗**TRAILHEAD:** **Simsbury, CT.** FCHT parking on Hopmeadow St.

DIRECTIONS SOUTH? Go to the Rail Trail Guide at the end of this chapter.

PARKING ACCESS:

Avon

- Trailhead GPS: Parking at 70 Simsbury Rd, ZIP 06001and also at Sperry Park along the FCHT (off Mountain View Ave).

- In Avon, various parking areas in Avon Center.

Simsbury

- Trailhead GPS: Parking at 1110 Hopmeadow St (intersection of Ely Ln/Hopmeadow St), ZIP 06070.

- Parking at Curtiss Park off 62 Tariffville Rd/CT-315. Curtiss Park has parking plus a picnic area, athletic fields, fishing, canoeing and camping is available.

- Trail parking at the end of Lordship Rd off Wolcott Rd.

- Parking is available at Simsbury Shops along Hopmeadow St/CT-10/202 and Tariffville Rd/CT-315.

- Public parking between Iron Horse Blvd and Simsbury Shops right next to the Farmington Canal Heritage Trail (park here and easily bike north or south).

- Trailhead GPS at 10 Winslow St off US-202/10/ Hopmeadow St.

- Small parking lot on Old Canal Way across from 200 Hopmeadow St on CT-10/US-202.

SIMSBURY HISTORY

Before settlers came up the Farmington River (in 1640) to settle the area now called Simsbury, native Indians from the Massacoe Tribe lived off the land because the valley had plenty of game and workable land. Gradually Indian lands were sold (or maybe taken by force) to early English settlers. Indian issues caused King Philip (Chief Metacom) to attack local settlers (Metacom was the son of Massasoit, the Indian Chief that befriended the Pilgrims). The conflict was over in circa 1676. Simsbury is famous for having the first steel mill in America and locally, copper was discovered in the mountains along the Talcott Mountain range which later became the site of the New-Gate Prison, a Revolutionary War Prison. Simsbury takes great pride in maintaining its historical Farmington Valley small town charm. Evidence of this abounds when you take a bicycle ride around town.

SIMSBURY CANAL HISTORY

Where's the canal? In Simsbury, the canal, CT-10/US-202 and the rail road bed zigzag back and forth all the way to the East Granby border. The rail trail follows the rail bed most of the way.

Canal History: It's interesting to note that as the canal winds around hills and valleys east of the Farmington River, not one canal lock was ever built. However, several culverts do exist to allow horse and buggy traffic over the canal (a culvert is defined as a bridge over water). At this point in time, as noted by Charles Harte, "The 'Westfield Register' of July 1, 1829, reported the canal in use from New Haven to Simsbury, operation above that point being prevented by the unfinished rebuilding of the Salmon Brook Arch". Remnants of the Hop Brook Arch, partially destroyed by the 1955 flood, may still be seen across from 640 Hopmeadow St.

A preserved section of the canal can be found on Old Canal Way across from 200 Hopmeadow St on CT-10/US-202. Follow Old Canal Way until you come to a small parking lot, park your car or bike and take a moment and walk along the canal for a short distance and imagine that you are walking along leading a horse or two all the way to Northampton or New Haven.

The canal is about 26 miles long as it passes through Simsbury from Southington to Granby still on the "Long Level". In addition, as noted elsewhere, the canal was 46′ wide at the top and 20′ at the bottom with a depth of about 6′. The tow path where horses pulled barges or packet boats was 10′ wide and the opposite berm was 7′ wide rising 2′ above the top of the water. An amazing feat when you realize the canal was hand made by man and mule.

SIMSBURY RAIL TRAIL

A good example of the way the canal looked back in 1800's when packet boats worked the canal from New Haven to Northampton. When on the Farmington Canal Heritage Trail in Simsbury, you will be able to see the old canal. The trail passes over the street named Old Canal Way (parallel to Route 202/10 – see map). Watercolor by Robert R. Madison

Author on the towpath the way it looks today on the preserved Simsbury Old Canal Way.

CANAL RAILROAD

Where's the railroad? The railroad, CT-10/US-202 and the canal zigzag back and forth in Simsbury toward the East Granby border.

Railroad History: In 1846 the New Haven & Northampton RR (NH&N) started construction in Simsbury and ultimately connected to Granby in 1850. In 1869 the railroad was operated by NY&NH ultimately to be run by NHRR. The railroad was abandoned in 1976 to become the Farmington Valley Greenway rail-trail.

A small part of the Canal Railroad, south of Granby, was built by the Connecticut Western Rail Road (CWRR) as to be an extension of its main connection to Hartford ultimately becoming the Central New England RR (CNERR) in 1898. Today the Brook Trail follows its path. This small segment was abandoned in 1968.

Simsbury Railroad Depot on Railroad Street. This circa 1874 building was designed in the Italianate Style. The station is now on the National Register of Historic Places. Behind the little replica of a steam engine is a real caboose. The original tracks in the foreground can still be seen in this photo.

BICYCLE REPAIR AND RENTAL FACILITIES

Bicycle Cellar
532 Hopmeadow St
Simsbury, CT
203 658-1311
www.bicyclecellar.com

Ridgeline Bikes of Avon
175 W Main St
Avon, CT 06001
860 676-8800

OFF RAIL TRAIL EXCURSIONS

(Excursions may or may not require bicycles)

1. Simsbury Town Hall
933 Hopmeadow St
Simsbury, CT 06070
860 658-3200
www..simsbury-ct.gov

2. Talcott Mountain State Park
(CT-185/560 Simsbury Rd)

3. Simsbury Historical Society
800 Hopmeadow St
Simsbury, CT 06070
860 658-2500
www.infor@simsburyhistory.org

4. Shopping plazas or malls are adjacent to the trail on US-10/ Hopmeadow St

5. A classic example of how the canal was excavated on level ground can be found in the preserved section of the canal on Old Canal Way across from 200 Hopmeadow St.

Metacomet Trail

Simbsury Farms
(100 Old Farms Rd)

Heublein Tower
(CT-185)

Pinchot Park
(CT-185/Hartford Rd)

Schulz Park
(US-10/921 Hopmeadow St)

Curtis Park
(CT-315/Tariffville Rd)

Great Pond
(Great Pond Rd)

Penwood State Park
(CT-185/170 Hartford Rd)

West Mountain Park
(West Mountain Rd)

Stratton Brook State Park
(CT-185)

Town Forest Park
(Town Forest Rd)

Weatogue Park
(US-10)

Simsbury Free Library
(749 Hopmeadow St)

RAIL TRAIL GUIDE

	NORTH	HEADING SOUTH
MILES N		MILES S
6.6	⊗ **TRAILHEAD @** Simsbury, Hopmeadow Street	0
	→ On Hopmeadow, right onto FCHT.	0.1
	→ Right on FCHT.	2.1
	→ Right on Drake Hill Rd. and the FCHT.	0.1
	← Left onto FCHT until reaching Hopmeadow St..	1.7
	↑ On FCHT passing Winslow Pl. and crossing Hopmeadow St.	0.1
	← Left on FCHT.	2.4
	→ Enter FCHT From Simsbury Rd./Mountain View Ave./Fisher Rd or Sperry Park. 0.1 mi	0.1
0.1	← Left on Hopmeadow St and Trailhead.	
2.1	→ Right on FCHT.	
0.1	← Left on Drake Hill Rd. still on FCHT.	
1.7	← Left on FCHT.	
0.1	↑ Crossing Winslow Pl. back right onto FCHT.	
2.4	↑ Continue on FCHT to Hopmeadow intersection.	
0.1	↑ Enter FCHT From Simsbury Rd./Mountain View Ave./Fisher Rd or Sperry Park. 0.1 mi	
0	⊗ **TRAILHEAD @** Avon, Sperry Park.	6.6
HEADING NORTH	SOUTH	

SECTION 9: EAST GRANBY
(FARMINGTON CANAL)

Common Names: East Coast Greenway and Farmington Canal

Route: Simsbury Tariffville Rd (Curtiss Park) to East Granby Hartford Ave (Granbrook Park).

Total Distance: 4.2 miles or 25 - 40 minutes.

Ride Details: Skill level is easy to moderate. Elevation gain is minimal except when on Granbrook Park Rd (hill approach).

Significant Canal Features: North of Cranbrook Park off Hartford Ave, the 40' Salmon Brook Culvert spanned the Salmon Brook (finished in 1829 in the then Granby, CT). In 1858 East Granby became incorporated. In today's East Granby, Holcomb's Basin was the 'Port of Granby' a significant home dockage for Granby's canal boats.

Grandson Jacob Roderiques and Grandfather Hoyt Willis on the rail trail near Lake Basile (a nearby signpost directs the bicyclist to discover the remnants of the old canal that stretches 86 miles from New Haven, CT to Northampton, MA).

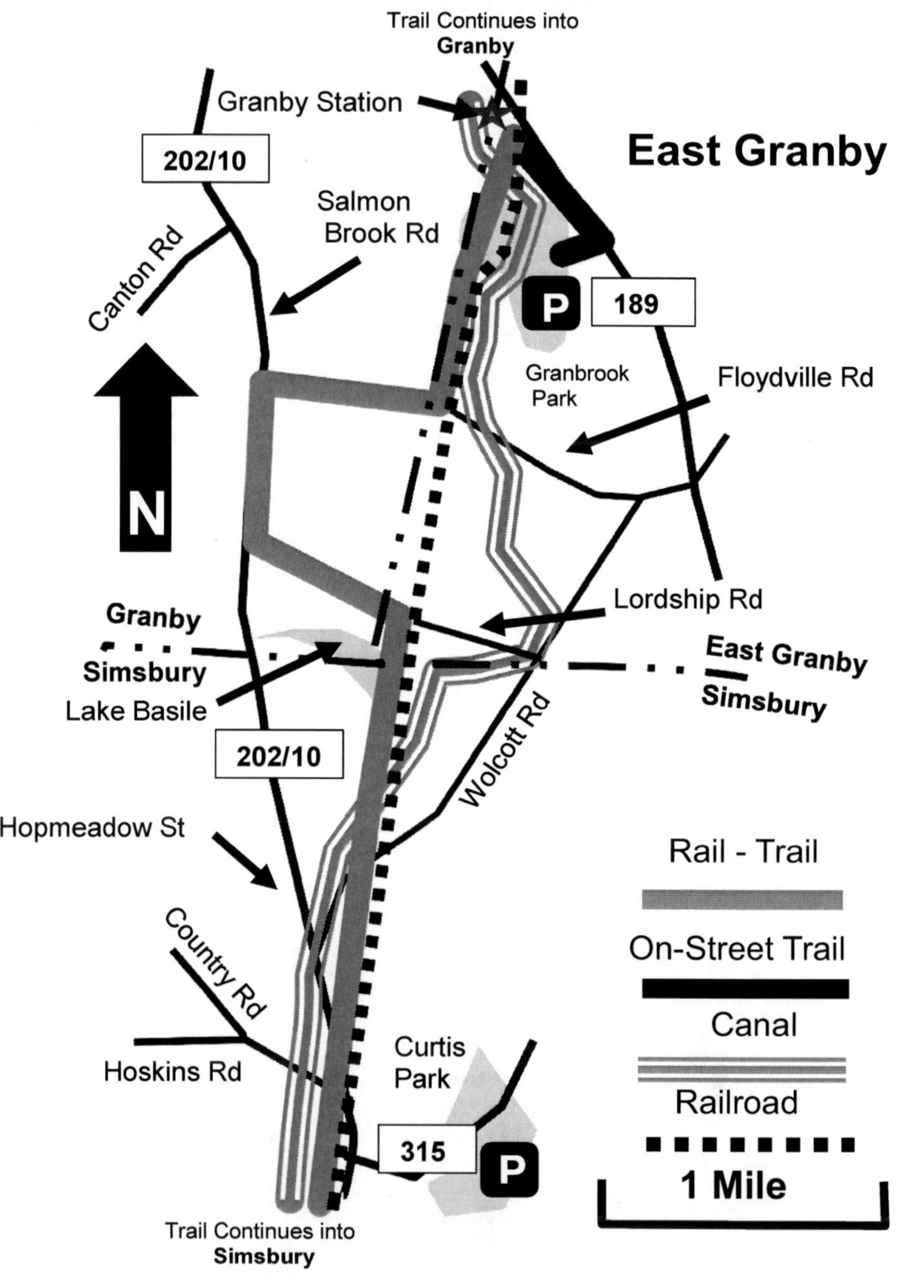
EAST GRANBY RAIL TRAIL MAP
Trail Continues into
Granby
Granby Station
202/10
East Granby
Salmon
Brook Rd
Canton Rd
P
189
Granbrook
Park
Floydville Rd
N
Lordship Rd
Granby
Simsbury
East Granby
Simsbury
Lake Basile
202/10
Wolcott Rd
Hopmeadow St
Rail - Trail
On-Street Trail
Country Rd
Canal
Hoskins Rd
Curtis
Park
Railroad
315
P
1 Mile
Trail Continues into
Simsbury

FARMINGTON CANAL RAIL TRAIL
EAST GRANBY RAIL TRAIL

RAIL TRAIL:

⊗**TRAILHEAD:** Simsbury, CT. FCHT parking on 1110 Hopmeadow St, (In Simsbury, CT, south of East Granby, CT where parking is convenient).

← From the trailhead, turn left and head north on FCHT following Hopmeadow St/CT-10/US-202 toward Tariffville Rd. 1.4 mi.

← Still on FCHT, take a left at Lordship Rd Follow FCHT until reaching Salmon Brook St (you are paralleling Salmon Brook St, leaving the original rail bed). 1.0 mi.

→ Still on the FCHT, take a right at the junction of Salmon Brook St and Floydville Rd traveling 0.5 mi.

← Left on FCHT (just before Railroad Ave). 0.8 mi.

→ Sharp right on the FCHT at the junction of CT-189/Harford Ave 0.3 mi.

→ Taking another right onto Granbrook Park Rd (parking at the bottom of the hill). 0.2 mi.

⊗**TRAILHEAD:** **East Granby, CT** Parking at Granbrook Park off CT-189/ Hartford Ave.

DIRECTIONS SOUTH? Go to the Rail Trail Guide at the end of this chapter.

PARKING ACCESS:

Simsbury

- Trailhead GPS: Parking at 1110 Hopmeadow St (intersection of Ely Ln/Hopmeadow St), ZIP 06070

• Parking at Curtiss Park off 62 Tariffville Rd/CT-315. Curtiss Park has parking plus a picnic area, athletic fields, fishing, canoeing and camping is available.

• Trail parking at the end of Lordship Rd off Wolcott Rd.

• Parking is available at Simsbury Shops along Hopmeadow St/CT-10/202 and Tariffville Rd/CT-315.

• Public parking between Iron Horse Blvd and Simsbury Shops right next to the Farmington Canal Heritage Trail (park here and easily bike north or south)

East Granby

• Trailhead GPS: 19 Granbrook Road, ZIP 06026.

• Parking at Granbrook Park off CT- 189 on Hartford Ave 0.1 mi south of trail (vehicle/bicycle parking).

• End of Lordship Rd off Wolcott Rd.

• CT-10/CT-189/Salmon Brook St on-street.

BICYCLE REPAIR AND RENTAL FACILITIES

Bicycle Repairs Express
Serving the Granby Area
860 808-9966

New England Bicycle
549 College Hwy
Southwick, MA, 01077
413 569-1874
www.newenglandbicycle.com

Ridgeline Bikes Of Avon
175 W Main St
Avon, CT 06001
860 676-8800

EAST GRANBY HISTORY

East Granby is split by the Peak Mountain range or Copper Mountain Range. In fact, it sits in the middle of a basalt ridged mountain with Granby to the west and Windsor Locks to the east with Simsbury just below it. As early as 1790, East Granby wanted to become its own town. In 1858 East Granby finally became incorporated as a separate town! A copper mine existed west of the Talcott Range (now part of the Newgate Prison - a Revolutionary War jail). And, Turkey Hill Rd (Route 20) was named after the Turkey Hills Parish Society, a Congregational Parish. Dairy products and tobacco made up the major source of revenue during the early settlement years in East Granby.

EAST GRANBY CANAL HISTORY

Where's the canal? The canal meanders following the contours along the rail trail route for less than a few miles (the total length of the rail trail in East Granby is about 5 miles). The canal and the rail trail/railroad bed only coincide at the southernmost border of East Granby and the south of CT-189/Hartford Ave (near Lake Basile signpost on the rail trail).

Canal History: A canal packet boat can travel some 26 miles from East Granby to Southington's Lock 7 without wasting time moving up or down in a lock (the 'Long Level' passed through Southington, Plainville, Farmington, Avon, Simsbury and East Granby). The high 40' Salmon Brook Culvert was built in 1828 and spanned the Salmon Brook just north of Cranbrook Park off Hartford Ave (just south of the Old Granby Railway Station).

In the fall of 1831, a drought lowered the water in Congamond Lake to such an extent that traffic stopped for three months and subsequently a feeder line was constructed from Salmon Brook (before East Granby separated from Granby).

Arches were built over rivers and brooks. In this case, during heavy rains, if debris blocked the water flow, a huge dam is created and everything washes away. This arch washed away many times and in 1934 it disappeared. Watercolor by Robert R Madison

This photo taken in 1933 by Charles Rufus Harte of the Salmon Brook Arch or Culvert. It was built in 1828 in then Granby. Canal boats could go over or under arches but only over aqueducts.

CANAL RAILROAD

Restored Granby Station on the rail-trail in today's East Granby

Where's the railroad? The railroad and the rail trail are one and the same most of the time (except between Lordship Rd/Floydville Rd where the rail trail departs from the original railroad bed).

Railroad History: In 1846 the New Haven & Northampton RR (NH&N) started construction in Simsbury and ultimately connected to Granby in 1850. In 1869 the railroad was operated by NY&NH ultimately to be run by NHRR. An excellent example of the restored Old Granby Railway Station exists just north of Cranbrook Park at the intersection of Hartford Ave and the existing rail trail. The railroad was abandoned in 1976 and became the Farmington Valley Greenway Rail-Trail. A small part of the Canal Railroad, south of Granby, was built by the Connecticut Western Rail Road (CWRR) to be an extension of its main connection to Hartford ultimately becoming the Central New England RR (CNERR) in 1898. Today the Brook Trail follows the rail bed path. This small segment was abandoned in 1968.

OFF RAIL TRAIL EXCURSIONS

(Excursions may or may not require bicycles)

1. Lake Basile is located along the Farmington Canal Rail Trail in East Granby. A trailside sign says *"Farmington Canal, 1828 – 1848, Looking north, you can see the remnants of the canal. It crosses over Floydville Road and proceeds over Salmon Brook. To your left is Lake Basile. Cross over the bridge and to the left and up the hill you will see more remnants of the canal. Total distance from New Haven, Ct. to Northampton, Mass. Is 88 miles."*

2. East Granby Town Hall
9 Center St
East Granby, CT 05026
860 653-2576
www.eastgranbyct.org

3. Refer to Lake Basile Association for events.
www.LakeBasile.org

4. East Granby Historical Society
79 North Main St
East Granby, CT 05026
www.eastgranby.com/historicalsociety

East Granby Farms
(CT-187/79 N Main St)

Granbrook Park
(CT-189/Hartford Rd)

Cowles Park
(CT-187/S Main St)

Tariffville Gorge
(Tunxis Ave)

Metacomet Trail
(intersection CT-20/Newgate Rd)

Old Newgate Prison
(Newgate Rd)

Holcombs Basin
(CT-189/Hartford Rd)

East Granby Public Library
(24 Center St).

RAIL TRAIL GUIDE

	NORTH	HEADING SOUTH
MILES N		MILES S
4.2	⊗ **TRAILHEAD** @East Granby, Granbrook Park.	0
	← Granbrook Park via Granbrook Park Rd turning left at the junction of CT-189/Hartford Ave.	0.2
	← Turn left on CT-189/Hartford Ave taking a sharp left onto the FCHT.	0.3
	→ FHCT traveling south take a right upon reaching Floydville Rd.	0.8
	← After the right, continue west along the FHCT until arriving at Salmon Brook St and take a left.	0.5
	← At CT-10/US-202/Salmon Brook St go left until arriving at Lordship Rd bearing slightly right.	1.0
	→ Follow FCHT until reaching trailhead until reaching trailhead at the intersection of Ely Ln/Hopmeadow St on your right.	1.4
0.2	→ Right and parking at the bottom of the hill.	
0.3	→ At CT-189/Hartford Ave take a sharp right and continue until you see the entrance to Granbrook Park. Turn right.	
0.8	← Left on FCHT before Railroad Ave.	
0.5	→ Right at junctioin of Salmon Brooks St and Floydville Rd.	
1.0	← Left on FCHT at the junction of Lordship Rd. continuing all the way to Floydville Rd.	
1.4	← Left and head north on FCHT following Hopmeadow St/CT-10/US-202 toward Tariffville Rd.	
0	⊗ **TRAILHEAD** @ Simsbury, Hopmeadow Street.	4.2
HEADING NORTH	SOUTH	

NOTES

SECTION 10: GRANBY
(FARMINGTON CANAL)

Common Names: East Coast Greenway and Farmington Canal

Route: East Granby (Granbrook Park) to West Suffield Phelps Rd and Quarry Rd.

Total Distance: 4.8 miles or 30 - 45 minutes.

Ride Details: Skill level is easy to moderate. Elevation gain is minimal except near Granbrook Park Rd.

Significant Canal Features: Heading south, six abandoned locks (Locks 1 – 6) located above and below Hartford Ave/CT-189 are no longer visible. Lock 1, when filled with water, was 220 feet above sea level. These locks were originally made of wood and measured 80′ long and 12′ wide.

Bicyclists southbound on the Canal Greenway in Granby, CT.

GRANBY RAIL TRAIL MAP

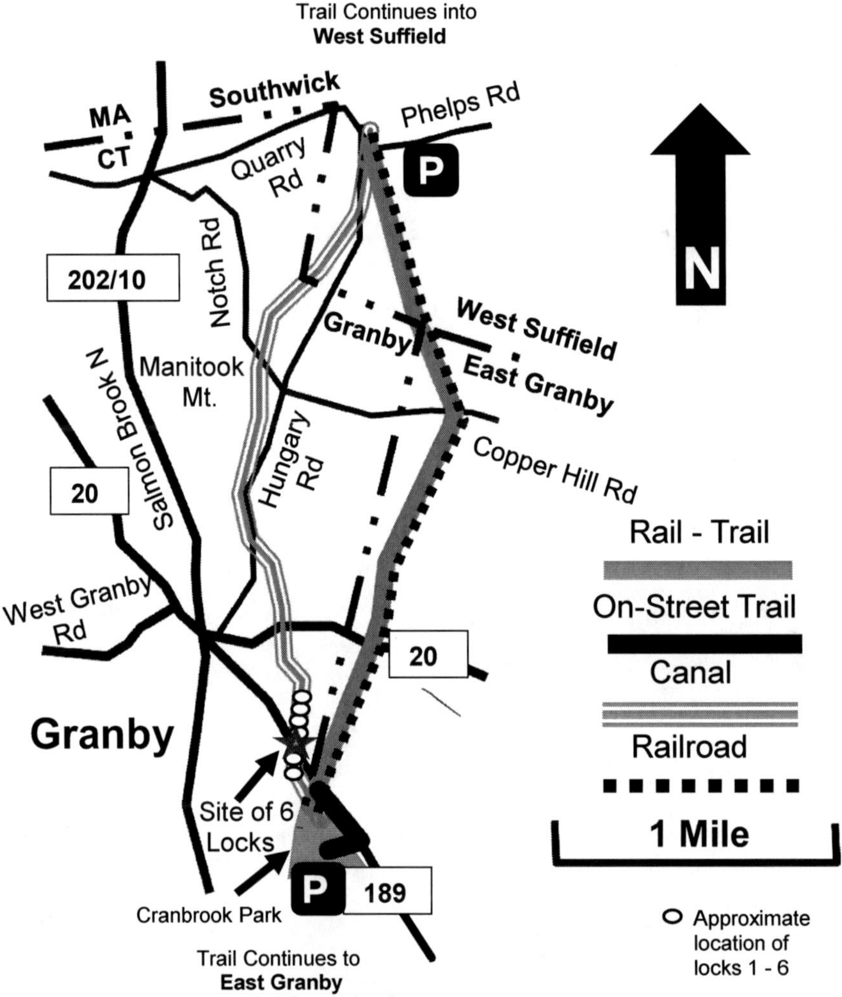

FARMINGTON CANAL

Note: The rail trail and the railroad pictured above are entirely within East Granby borders; however, the historic canal works its way in and around Manitook Mountain which is in Granby Connecticut.

GRANBY RAIL TRAIL

RAIL TRAIL:

⊗**TRAILHEAD:** East Granby, CT. Parking at Granbrook Park off CT- 189/ Hartford Ave.

↑ On Granbrook Park Rd 0.2 mi

← Left on CT-189/Hartford Ave 0.3 mi.

→ Right turn onto the Farmington Canal Heritage Trail. 4.3 mi.

↑ Arrive at the intersection of Phelps Rd and Quarry Rd (convenient parking not available in Granby next to the rail trail).

⊗**TRAILHEAD:** West Suffield, CT. Parking junction of Phelps Rd and Quarry Rd.

DIRECTIONS SOUTH? Go to the Rail Trail Guide at the end of this chapter.

PARKING ACCESS:

<u>East Granby</u>

- Trailhead GPS: 19 Granbrook Road, ZIP 06026.
- Parking at Granbrook Park off CT-189 on Hartford Ave 0.1 mi south of trail (vehicle/bicycle parking).
- Midway parking at junction of FCHT and Copper Hill Rd.
- Midway parking at junction of FCHT and CT-20/Turkey Hills Rd.

<u>West Suffield</u>

- Trailhead GPS: 5000 Phelps Road, ZIP 06093.
- Parking junction of Phelps Rd and Quarry Rd, West Suffield, CT.

GRANBY HISTORY

Settlers of early colonial Granby were Puritans. Like many other Connecticut communities seeking religious freedom during those early periods, Granby settlers also sought freedom from English religious tyranny. Settling in the wilderness west of the Connecticut River in the 17th century, families built homes and farms between the two branches of the Salmon Brook and this isolation separated their little community from neighbors; however, they, like other settlements, had to protect themselves from marauding Native Americans.

The land may have been good for religious freedom but it was not necessarily good farmland. In the mid eighteen hundreds, Granby developed water-powered manufacturing; however, steam-powered factories and floods made manufacturing difficult. Granby during this time period was Hartford County's leading cider distilling area.

The Town of Granby was incorporated in 1786 from Simsbury and East Granby was incorporated in 1858, several years after the canal ceased to carry traffic.

GRANBY CANAL HISTORY

Where's the canal? The canal does not follow the rail trail/railroad bed until you actually see the canal just south of Congamond Lake (the remainder of the canal somewhat follows the contours along the base of Manitook Mountain south of the lake).

Canal History: "To Granby belongs the place where on Monday, July 4th, 1825, ground was first broken for the Farmington Canal. . . It is estimated that between two and three thousand people were present and witnessed the removal of the first shovelful of earth as a starter of this important enterprise...after which a small hole was dug and the party returned to Salmon Brook in Granby, there to partake of a sumptuous repast on the village green." This comment came from an article on "The Old Farmington Canal" *The Cheshire-Hamden Times*, March 15, 1923. Other reports claim that Granby holds the distinction of having the first shovel full of dirt to start construction of the canal (in this marshy area south of Congamond Lake, even Southwick could claim the first shovel full of dirt if they wanted to).

Water within the canal drains in a southerly direction from the Upper Salmon Brook and the Congamond Lake in Southwick. Thus begins the 28 lock trek to the Long Island Sound. The bicyclist will observe the canal's 20 foot width first hand while traveling north of Granby (just before Congamond Lake). Of interest are the six locks just southeast of the center of Granby off CT-189 portrayed in the watercolor painting below. Each wooden lock was 80 feet long and 12 feet wide and operated by the Holcomb brothers. These 6 locks raised canal boats some 37' to meet the great Congamond Lake Summit or Southwick Pond Summit (as noted earlier, some 220 feet above sea level). Located just south of these six locks is the Salmon Brook Arch Culvert built in 1828. A picture taken by Charles Rufus Harte in 1933 dramatically portrays this arch (see page 130).

Granby's canal enthusiast Carl E. Walter (a Granby resident) deserves special recognition for his contributions in developing the 'Map of the Farmington Canal'; the completion of the 'Map of the Hampshire & Hampden Canal' and his many lectures to inform and enlighten history buffs.

Just down the hill from the restored Granby Station off CT-189 is the sight of Granby's six locks (on the left is Salmon Brook). These six locks have long since vanished. Watercolor by Robert R Madison

Photo of nearby Holcomb's Basin in 1933. A basin allows boats to pass while other boats unload or park. Photo by Charles Rufus Harte.

CANAL RAILROAD

Where's the railroad? The railroad and the rail trail follow each other.

Railroad History: "In April 1850 the Canal Railroad main line reached Salmon Brook in Granby, Connecticut, twenty miles beyond Plainville." Then trouble started because the major shareholder, Joseph Sheffield had begun grading to the Massachusetts state line north of Granby when the project swiftly ground to a halt: the Hartford & New Haven Railroad had filed a court injunction." The Hartford & New Haven (H&NH) was afraid the New York & New Haven (NY&NH) would surround Hartford thereby diverting revenue from the Connecticut River communities. The legal obstacle was an 1850 traffic agreement prohibiting the NY&NH from going beyond Granby. The Farmington Valley Railroad was ultimately chartered to build a section from Granby to the Massachusetts state line in 1852.

Current rail-trail trestle on the original footprint of the railroad trestle over Salmon Brook in what is now in East Granby (picture taken at Cranbrook Park).

BICYCLE REPAIR AND RENTAL FACILITIES

Granby Bicycle
29 Granby Farms Rd
Granby, CT 06035
860 653-4800

Bicycle Repairs Express
Serving the Granby Area
860 808-9966

New England Bicycle
549 College Hwy
Southwick, MA 01077
413 569-1874
www.newenglandbicycle.com

Ridgeline Bikes Of Avon
175 W Main St
Avon, CT 06001
860 676-8800

OFF RAIL TRAIL EXCURSIONS

(Excursions may or may not require bicycles)

1. Granby Town Hall
15 North Granby Rd
Granby, CT 06035
860 844-5308
www.granby-ct.gov

2. Salmon Brook Park
(215 Salmon Brook St)

3. Salmon Brook Historical Society
208 Salmon Brook St
Granby, CT
860 653-9713
www.salmonbrookhistorical.org

4. Old Granby Railroad Station
at corner of FCHT and CT-189/Hartford Ave

Granby Public Library
(15 N Granby Rd)

McLean Game Refuge
(US-10/202/Salmon Brook Rd & 150 Barndoor Hills Rd)

RAIL TRAIL GUIDE

NORTH

MILES N		HEADING SOUTH MILES S
4.8	⊗ **TRAILHEAD** @ West Suffield, Phelps Road.	0
	↑ At Phelps Rd, travel south on the Farmington Canal Heritage Trail.	4.3
	← Turn left onto Ct-189/Hartford Ave.	0.3
	→ Turn right onto Granbrook Park Rd. and continue down the hill to Granbrook Park.	0.2
4.3	→ Turn right on the Farmington Canal Heritage Trail.	
0.3	← Turn left on CT-189/Hartford Ave traveling west to the Farmington Canal Heritage Trail on your right.	
0.2	↑ Granbrook Part biking along Granbrook Park Rd to CT-168/Hartford Rd.	
0	⊗ **TRAILHEAD @** East Granby, Granbrook. Park	4.8
HEADING NORTH		

SOUTH

NOTES

SECTION 11: SUFFIELD
(FARMINGTON CANAL)

Common Name: East Coast Greenway, Farmington Canal and Southwick Rail-Trail.

Route: West Suffield Phelps Rd and Quarry Rd to Southwick Miller Rd.

Total Distance: 1.6 miles or 10 minutes.

Ride Details: Skill level is easy to moderate. Elevation gain is minimal. Some seating is available along the rail trail.

Significant Canal Features: A 'guard lock' to prevent water from accidentally draining Congamond Lake is located on the Connecticut/ Massachusetts border.

A photo of hikers on the West Suffield and Southwick rail-trail greenway at the junction of Connecticut and Massachusetts.

SUFFIELD RAIL TRAIL MAP

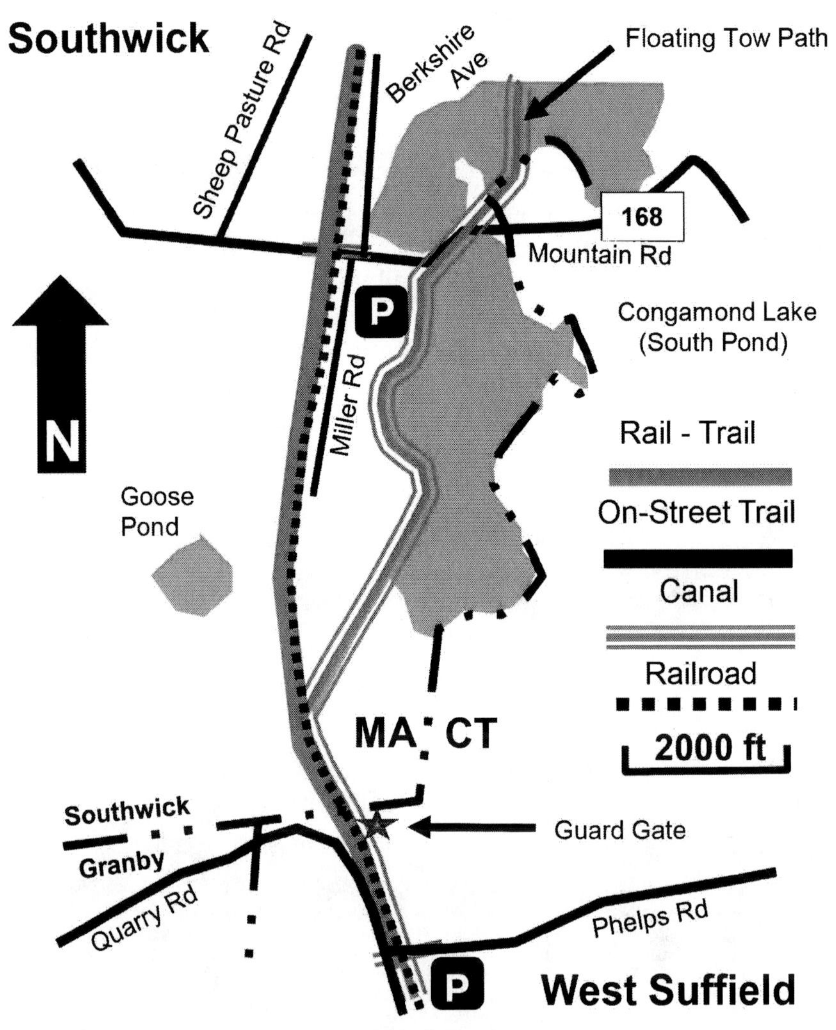

FARMINGTON CANAL TRAIL

SUFFIELD RAIL TRAIL

RAIL TRAIL:

⊗**TRAILHEAD** West Suffield, CT. Parking junction of Phelps Rd and Quarry Rd, West Suffield, CT.

↑ Head north on the FCHT to CT/MA border. 0.4 mi.

↑ Continue north 1.2 mi. to MA-168/ Congamond Rd and Miller Rd, Southwick, MA.

⊗**TRAILHEAD** Southwick, MA. Parking on Miller Rd at the junction of MA-168/Congamond Rd.

DIRECTIONS SOUTH? Go to the Rail Trail Guide at the end of this chapter.

PARKING ACCESS:

West Suffield, CT

- Trailhead GPS: 5000 Phelps Road, ZIP 06093.
- Parking junction of Phelps Rd and Quarry Rd, West Suffield, CT.

Southwick MA

- Trailhead GPS: 1 Miller Road, ZIP 01077.
- Parking on Miller Rd at the junction of MA-168/ Congamond Rd.

SUFFIELD HISTORY

Suffield stretches from the Connecticut River south of Springfield all the way over the Manitook Mountain Range to Congamond Lake. The settlement started in 1670 by Springfield, Massachusetts Major John Pynchon who paid the local tribe thirty English pounds for a tract of land known as Stony Brook. Suffield was part of Massachusetts for 79 years until it merged with Connecticut in 1749. Most of Suffield resides east of the mountain range in a typical New England setting with many historical houses whereas, over the mountain range, in the west, the West Suffield settlement is where farming (mainly tobacco) and water recreation (Congamond Lake) is the community's main source of revenue.

SUFFIELD CANAL HISTORY

Where's the canal? The canal in West Suffield is right next to the rail trail crossing over the rail trail just north of Phelps Rd. The Congamond Lake towpath stays mostly on the Southwick side of the lake; however, a short cut was made through a peninsula near Mountain Rd on the West Suffield side of the lake.

Canal History: The canal hugs the east side of Manitook Mountain which is in West Suffield. The canal, south of Congamond Lake, was a logical place to build a canal. Water feeding the Connecticut side of the canal came mainly from a feeder line rather than the Congamond Lake. The feeder line connected Salmon Brook to the canal (a guard gate prevented high water from entering the canal – the rail trail goes over this gate just south of the state border). Much of the canal can still be seen along the rail trail. The canal is 20′ wide at the bottom and 34′ to 36′ wide at the surface. In addition, the towpath itself is at least 10′ wide and not more than 5′ above the water's surface. The opposite bank from the towpath could not be less than 2′ above the water's surface.

Charles Harte, in his report on Connecticut Canals to the Connecticut Society of Engineers commented that "In 1838 a new line of packet boats was started. Making the trip between New Haven and Northampton at the previously only dreamed of time of 24 hours for the trip, - they left, and arrived, at least by the time-table, at 3 p.m. – and charging but $3.75 for passage and food, they represented the last word in canal transportation."

Canal packet leaving the guard gate as it begins to enter Congamond Lake. Watercolor by Robert R. Madison

2013 photo of author and lecturer Carl E. Walter surrounded by canal enthusiasts on the original towpath/railroad bed/rail-trail in West Suffield, CT.

CANAL RAILROAD

Where's the railroad? The railroad and the rail trail are one and the same most of the time for the short distance in West Suffield.

Rail trail overpass over original NH&N railroad abutments on Phelps Rd.

Railroad History: In 1846 the New Haven & Northampton RR (NH&N) started construction in Simsbury and ultimately connected to Granby in 1850. In 1869 the railroad was operated by NY&NH ultimately to be run by NHRR. The railroad was abandoned in 1976 and became the Farmington Valley Greenway rail-trail. West Suffield did not have a railroad depot; however, Granby and Southwick sidings were used for freight or passengers. The West Suffield Mountain Range was a major transportation barrier between West Suffield and Suffield.

BICYCLE REPAIR AND RENTAL FACILITIES

New England Bike & Scuba
526 College Hwy
Southwick, MA 01077
413 569-1874
www.nebikeandscuba.com

OFF RAIL TRAIL EXCURSIONS

(Excursions may or may not require bicycles)

1. Suffield Town Hall
83 Mountain Rd
Suffield, CT 06078
860 668-3880
www.suffieldtownhall.com

2. Sunrise Park & Stoneybrook Park
(2075 Mountain Rd)

3. Suffield Historical Society
King House Museum
232 South Main St. 06078
860 668-5256
www.suffieldhistoricalsociety.org

Bazin Bruce Memorial Park
(1100 Sheldon St)

Babbs Park
(433 Babbs Rd)

King House Museum
(232 S Main St)

Kent Memorial Library
(50 N Main St)

RAIL TRAIL GUIDE

	NORTH	HEADING SOUTH
MILES N		MILES S
1.6	⊗ **TRAILHEAD** @ Southwick, Miller Road	0
	↑ Miller Rd to CT/MA border.	1.2
	↑ CT/MA border to Phelps Rd and Quarry Rd,	0.4
1.2	↑CT/MA border to Southwick, MA & Miller Rd.	
0.4	↑ Junction of Phelps Rd and Quarry Rd on Farmington Canal Heritage Trail (FCHT), head north to CT/MA border.	
0	⊗ **TRAILHEAD** @ West Suffield, Phelps Road	1.6
HEADING NORTH	SOUTH	

SECTION 12: SOUTHWICK
(SOUTHWICK RAIL TRAIL)

Common Names: East Coast Greenway, Southwick Rail Trail, Hampden & Hampshire Canal and New Haven – Northampton Railroad Greenway.

Route: Southwick Miller Rd. to Westfield Shaker Rd.

Total Distance: 5.2 miles. 30 - 45 minutes.

Ride Details: Skill level is easy. Elevation gain is minimal. Rest areas and a porta-potty may be available.

Significant Canal Features: A Guard Lock at the border of Connecticut/ Massachusetts was used to prevent draining of Congamond Lake: in addition to a dirt tow path and an abandoned 700′ wooden floating tow path; locks 1 – 8 dropped the water level down 68′ as the canal headed north to the Westfield town line.

A bicyclist on the Southwick Rail Trail with the canal to the left

SOUTHWICK RAIL TRAIL MAP

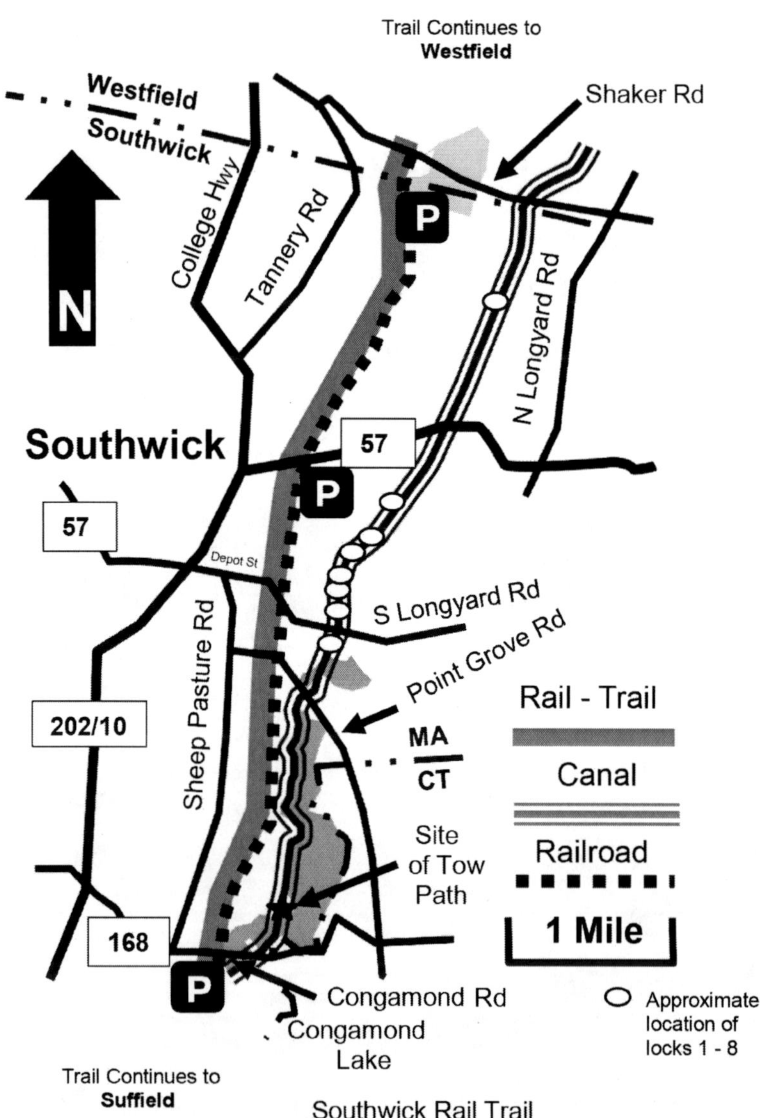

SOUTHWICK RAIL TRAIL

SOUTHWICK RAIL TRAIL

RAIL TRAIL:

⊗**TRAILHEAD**: Southwick, MA. Parking on Miller Road.

↑ From Miller Rd, get on the Southwick Rail Trail (SRT) traveling a short distance crossing MA-168/Congamond Rd.

↑ After crossing MA-168/Congamond Rd., on SRT, travel past the Depot Street intersection to MA-57/Feeding Hills Rd 3.1 mi.

↑ Still on the SRT, continue to Shaker Rd and rail trail parking. 1.8 mi. This is the beginning of the Colombia Greenway RailTrail.

⊗**TRAILHEAD**: Westfield, MA. Parking at the Colombia Greenway RailTrail parking lot on Shaker Road.

DIRECTIONS SOUTH? Go to the Rail Trail Guide at the end of this chapter.

PARKING ACCESS:

Southwick MA

- Trailhead GPS: 1 Miller Road, ZIP 01077.

- Junction MA-168/Congamond Rd and Miller Rd, follow signs for Southwick Rail Trail to vehicle/bicycle parking.

- Junction of Southwick Rail-Trail and MA-57/Feeding Hills Rd midway on-street parking or parking at nearby public schools.

Westfield, MA

- Trailhead GPS: 990 Shaker Road, ZIP 01086.

- Parking at the Colombia Greenway Rail Trail parking lot off Shaker Road.

SOUTHWICK HISTORY

In the early 1800's Southwick was largely a farming community with Congamond Lakes becoming a popular attraction in the late 1800's. Southwick was settled by households that moved south from Westfield, along the main north-south road now called College Highway or Route 10. Residents in the then southern part of Westfield petitioned on March 15, 1765 to become a separate town. Southwick, the south village or "wick" of Westfield became a district and in 1775, it became a full-fledged town. "In 1774, just before the outbreak of the American Revolution, the area known as the "Jog" became part of Simsbury, Connecticut, reducing the area of Southwick by one third. When the Salmon Brook area of Simsbury became the separate town of Granby in 1786, the "Jog" area was included. After the affairs of the war and new federal constitution were settled, it still took another several years before the "Jog" returned to Southwick and the jurisdiction of Massachusetts."

SOUTHWICK CANAL HISTORY

Where's the canal? The canal does not follow the rail trail until it reconnects to the rail bed in downtown Westfield. Instead the canal follows the contours of Congamond Lake meandering north and east of the rail trail hugging the hills well east of MA-10/US-202 and the rail trail.

Canal History: Construction of the Southwick section of the canal began in November 1, 1826. The canal section (then called the Hampden & Hampshire Canal) traveling north to Northampton started at the CT/MA state line and conversely, construction of the southern section (then called the Farmington Canal) of the canal started at the CT/MA state line in July, 1825 and headed south to New Haven, Connecticut. Just south of South Pond, on the trail, you will see water draining south into the canal and on to Granby, CT. This high point was known as the 'Southwick Pond Summit' because it is 220 feet above sea level (via locks the canal water drains north into Westfield). The other high point is 'Timber Swamp Summit' just north of Westfield and this part of the canal is 232 feet above sea level. Also, in this general area, as you are bicycling on or next to the tow path; maybe observe the location of the Guard Gate (the Guard Gate prevents accidental draining of the lake); the water feeder line from Palmer Brook and in the distance, Congamond Lake. At this junction, the tow path follows the western edge of Congamond Lake except for where it briefly passes along the eastern side onto Middle Pond where the 700 foot Floating Towpath (placed in position in September, 1828) once existed and rejoins the western side of Middle Pond as it makes its way to North Pond and Southwick's Lock 1 that connects to 7 other locks draining downwards to Westfield.

You cannot see these locks anymore. The flood of 1955 washed all remaining traces away. However, at the intersection of Depot St and Powder Mill Rd, a little down South Longyard Rd, one can see where the canal worked its way downward toward Westfield passing between Locks 1 & 2 (Locks 1 & 2 are located between South Longyard Rd). One can stand in the valley between the once existing locks and imagine the immensity of what the locking system must have looked like long ago. The Rail Trail does not follow the canal; the Rail Trail follows the original railroad tracks through the countryside and farmland. The Rail Trail picks up the canal in Westfield soon after the riding path crosses Little River. On page 164 in the next chapter, a bicyclist is passing the point where the canal intersects the Rail Trail again.

Painting of Locks 1, 2, 3 and 4 show the way the locks might have appeared when the canal was in operation. Lock 1 is at the top of the hill and lock 4 is at the bottom of the cut. The canal packet boat is headed north toward Locks 5 & 6 just off to the left in this painting. A huge cut was carved out of the hills in northern part of Congamond Lake (above and to the right of the painting) to allow boats to drop down to the lower level so they could be towed toward Westfield or upward onto the North Pond of the Congamond Lake. The above canal boat is some 40 feet below the levie of the Congamond Lakes. Watercolor by Robert R. Madison.

In the pamphlet published by the 1770 – 1970 Southwick Bicentennial Committee, they commented that "One section of the Canal where it connected with the North Pond was very easily located off South Longyard Road until the hurricane and flood of 1955. . . The hurricane of 1955 which brought torrential rains in this area caused the North Pond to burst through the mouth of the old canal carrying away a section of South Longyard Road and the homes of the Frank Jarry family, which was known as the 'old lock-house,' and the Bernard Drummond family".

After the 1955 hurricane and flood, the cut was filled in to a level many feet above the lake. Today, a road and houses can be seen on or over the old canal.

Photograph of the canal entrance/exit inside the canal just south of Congamond's South Pond (taken from the author's kayak looking north). Canal water from the Congamond Lakes drains south toward Granby via an existing waterway next to the rail-trail. A 'Guard Lock' can be seen next to the rail-trail just south of Southwick and West Suffield. The 'Guard Lock' prevents water from draining the lake.

CANAL RAILROAD

Southwick Depot (left) was located on the west side of Powder Mill Road (note: the Rail Trail cuts across the intersection of Depot/Powder Mill Road) and the picture on the right depicts the Congamond Depot (note: This depot was located near the marina next to the Rail Trail intersection on Congamond Road. Pictures courtesy of the Southwick Historical Society, Inc.

Where's the railroad? The railroad and the rail-trail follow each other through the eastern section of Southwick (the rail-trail parallels Congamond Lake).

Railroad History: From New Haven, town by town, the railroad was extended until by 1852 the Hampden Railroad Company (HRC) was chartered to build a railroad from Westfield to Southwick and the Connecticut State line near Granby, CT. Over time, different railroad lines owned, leased or chartered what was called 'the Old Canal Railroad' (the Farmington Valley Railroad and the Hampshire & Hampden Corporation were leased to the New Haven & Northampton Company in 1859 and in 1862 all lines were merged into the New Haven & Northampton Company to ultimately become the New York, New Haven and Hartford Railroad up to 1910) until the railroad was abandoned in 1976 and eventually became the Southwick Rail-Trail. Southwick had two railroad stations: One was located at the eastern end of Depot St. and the other, Congamond Station, was located near the lake on Congamond Road.

BICYCLE REPAIR AND RENTAL

New England Bike & Scuba
526 College Hwy
Southwick, MA 01077
413 569-1874
www.nebikeandscuba.com

OFF RAIL TRAIL EXCURSIONS

(Excursions may or may not require bicycles)

1. Southwick Town Hall
454 College Highway
Southwick, MA 01077
413 569-5504
www.southwickma.org

2. Congamond Lake
(93 Point Grove)

3. Pioneer Valley Live Steamers
(real steam engines on miniaturized track)
108 Hillside Rd
Southwick, MA 01077
www.pvls.org

4. Southwick History Museum
(Joseph Moore House-1751 & C.J. Gillett Cigar Factory/Warehouse-1872)
86-88 College Highway
www.southwickhistoricalsociety.org

5. Possible location of lock 1: Head east on S Longyard Rd 0.5 mile at the point where the Rail Trail crosses Depot St. until you reach a ravine and look north to lock 1 and south across the road to lock 2.

6. Canal view: At the intersection of the Rail Trail and Feeding Hills Rd/Rt-57 (you might find parking 0.3 mi east or west at the library or shopping center) if you bicycle east on the heavily traveled road for 0.3 mi, on your right you will see the Southwick Library and behind the library on the hill is the high school. Behind the high school is a parking lot and if you were to "bushwhack" and walk down into the woods you will find an excellent, untouched, example of what the historic canal looked like including tow path and all. This area is a classic example of how the canal was excavated in mountainous areas; that is, where possible, the canal was cut into the side of a hill with the earth from one side of the hill moved to the other side creating a trench (the canal) and a tow path at the same time.

Shopping plazas or malls exist on US-10/202/College Highway

Babbs Park
(433 Babbs Rd)

Southwick Public Library
(95 Feeding Hills Rd)

RAIL TRAIL GUIDE

NORTH

MILES N		HEADING SOUTH MILES S
5.2	⊗ **TRAILHEAD** @ Westfield, Shaker Road.	0
	↑ Shaker Rd Westfield, on the Columbia Greenway RailTrail (CGRT), continue north toward MA-57/Feeding Hills Rd.	1.9
	↑ From MA-57/Feeding Hills Rd continue to Southwick RailTrail (SRT) Miller St	3.3
1.9	↑ Still on SRT, from from Feeding Hills Rd/MA-57 to Columbia Greenway RailTrail, Shaker Road, Westfield.	
3.3	↑ Southwick RailTrail (SRT) Miller St to SRT Feeding Hills Rd/MA-57.	
0	⊗ **TRAILHEAD** @ Southwick, Miller Road.	5.2
HEADING NORTH		

SOUTH

NOTES

SECTION 13: WESTFIELD
(COLOMBIA GREENWAY RAIL TRAIL)

Common Names: East Coast Greenway, Colombia Greenway Rail Trail or Hampden/Hampshire Canal Rail Trail.

Routes: Westfield Shaker Rd to Westfield Brickyard/Valley Rd.

NOTE: Two routes outlined below allow the biker to go 'on street' to locate different sections of the canal rather than follow the Colombia Greenway Rail Trail. See Rail Trail description outlined below.

Total Distance: 7.9 miles or 35 - 50 minutes via Columbia Greenway Rail Trail Route or 9.6 miles or 60 - 90 minutes via the 'on street' canal route.

Ride Details: On Columbia Greenway Rail Trail: Skill level is easy to moderate. Elevation drops/rises at both ends. (NOTE: steep decline north of Shaker Rd).

'On Street' Canal Route: Ride Skill level is moderate 'plus' with very busy street travel. Elevation gain/loss is up and down at both ends of the trail. Care should be taken. The ride is flat downtown.

Significant Canal Features: Ten locks (9 - 18) were within Westfield's border. Lock 10 followed by locks 11 - 16 raising a northbound boat some 80' feet; then, locks 17 and 18 raised boats another 18' or 20'. In addition, three major aqueducts (80' Great Brook, 300' Little River and 330' Westfield River) carried canal boats over water. Two basins, one 'Port of Westfield' located on Main St and the second basin, North Basin, located just over the north side of the Great River Bridge. Several feeder lines fed the canal system. A feeder line over six miles long collected water from the Westfield River in Woronoco (Salmon Falls) and carried it to the canal just north of Lock 18 somewhat above where the current railroad tracks cross Lockhouse Rd. (see picture on following page).

This photograph shows the bike path crossing over the Pioneer Valley Railroad tracks on Lockhouse Road with Turnpike Industrial Road on the left. On the right side of this photograph canal Locks 16 and 17 once existed. Along this route, Locks 10 through 18 raised the level of the canal about 88 feet to the Northern Summit and on to Southampton.

To the immediate left of the bicyclist and telephone pole (just a little north of Silver Street) are some railroad ties. At this point the canal reconnects to the rail-trail after leaving the canal and railroad bed just south of Southwick's Congamond Lake.

WESTFIELD RAIL TRAIL MAP

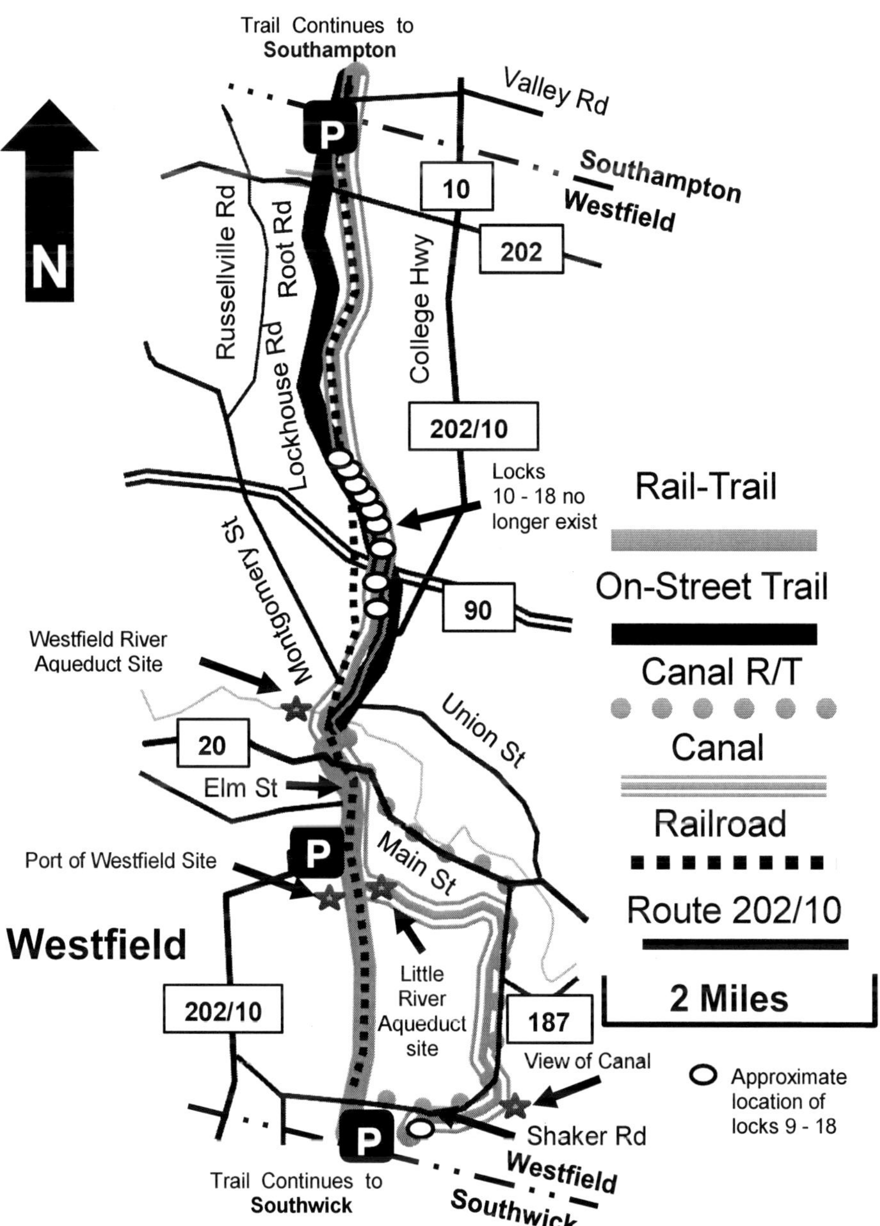

COLUMBIA GREENWAY RAIL TRAIL AND CANAL ROUTE

WESTFIELD RAIL TRAIL

RAIL TRAIL:

<u>Columbia Greenway Rail Trail</u>
7.9 miles or 40 - 50 minutes

⊗**TRAILHEAD:** <u>Westfield, MA</u>. Parking at the Colombia Greenway RailTrail parking lot on Shaker Road.

> *NOTICE: Until Westfield's Columbia Greenway Rail Trail is compete, bikers traveling north can follow the suggested route or follow the heavily traffic US-202/10 College Highway route from downtown Westfield to Southampton.*

↑ From the Columbia Greenway Rail Trail (CGRT), cross Shaker Rd toward Westfield to Main St. 2.1 mi.

↑ On CGRT, continue toward the Westfield River Bridge. 1.4 mi. (if construction, exit CGRT ← left on Main St exit and → right onto busy US-20/Main St/Elm St/US-202 toward the Westfield River Bridge. 0.8 mi.).

NOTE: The Colombia Greenway Rail Trail route follows the New York/ New Haven/Hartford railroad across Little River to downtown Westfield on an elevated railroad bed paralleling busy US-202/10/Elm St 2.0 mi. to the 'Great Bridge'. [At this point, the bicyclist picks up the Canal Route at the junction of the Westfield River or the 'Great Bridge].

↑ From the Westfield River Bridge, continue on busy US-202/10/Elm St to Lockhouse Rd 1.7. mi.

← Left onto Lockhouse Rd (NOTE: nine canal locks once existed here) until it becomes Root Rd [passing Summit Lock Rd on your right]). 2.4 mi.

↑ Root Rd becomes Brickyard Rd at the border of Westfield and Southampton. 0.3 mi.

⊗**TRAILHEAD** <u>Southampton, MA</u>. 'On street" parking in the vicinity of Brickyard Rd/Valley Rd.

RAIL TRAIL:

Canal Route
9.6 miles or 60 - 90 minutes

⊗**TRAILHEAD:** Westfield, MA. Parking at the Colombia Greenway RailTrail parking lot on Shaker Road.

→ From the Colombia Greenway Rail Trail continue right onto Shaker Rd to Canal Dr. (past Lock 9). 2.3 mi.

↑ Continue to US-187/Little River Rd. 0.7 mi.

← Left while on US-187/Little River Rd toward heavily traveled US-20/ East Main St. 1.2 mi.

→ Right onto Meadow St. 0.7 mi.

→ Right onto US-202/MA-10/Elm St from the Westfield River Bridge, continue on busy US-202/MA-10/Elm St to Lockhouse Rd. 1.7 mi.

← Left onto Lockhouse Rd (NOTE: nine canal locks once existed here) until it becomes Root Rd [passing Summit Lock Rd on your right]). 2.4 mi.

↑ Root Rd becomes Brickyard Rd at the border of Westfield and Southampton. 0.3 mi.

⊗**TRAILHEAD:** Southampton, MA. 'On street" parking in the vicinity of 215 Brickyard Rd & Valley Rd.

DIRECTIONS SOUTH? Go to the Rail Trail Guide at the end of this chapter.

PARKING ACCESS:

Westfield, MA

- Trailhead GPS: 990 Shaker Road, ZIP 01086.

• Parking at the Colombia Greenway RailTrail parking lot off Shaker Road.

• Mid-route mall parking or 'on street' parking next to the Columbia Greenway Rail Trail off the East Silver Street Rail Trail exit.

• Mid-route 'on street' parking along the canal route including downtown Westfield and the Westfield Shops along MA-20/East Main St in Westfield.

Southampton, MA

• Trailhead GPS: 215 Brickyard Road ('on-street'), ZIP 01073.

• Near the intersection of Brickyard/Valley roads, rail tracks are imbedded in the roadway.

• Parking 'on street' at the intersection of Brickyard Rd/ Valley Rd (quicker access from US-10/College Hwy along driving west along Valley Rd).

WESTFIELD HISTORY

Westfield was founded in 1669 along the Westfield River. Westfield was the western outpost of the Massachusetts Colony. Earlier Westfield was home to American Indians named Woronocos, part of the Pocumtucks tribe. The village was nestled in the foothills of the Berkshire Mountains. In 1765 Southwick, once part of Westfield became a separate town. In the early years, Westfield was mainly an agricultural community. Later, industry was introduced when bicycles, cigars and whips became the major items produced. In the 1800's, Westfield was known as the 'Whip City' because of the numerous buggy-whip makers in the city. Westfield was the 'big city' for settlements in the western hill towns where paper products were the major industries.

WESTFIELD CANAL HISTORY

Where's the canal? *NOTE: One can elect to follow the Colombia Greenway Rail Trail route or the on street route that parallels the original* *canal until both connect at the Westfield River.* Leaving the Congamond Lake, the canal drops via 8 locks in Southwick to lock 9 in Westfield (at the intersection of Shaker Road and Laro Road). The canal meanders about a mile east of MA-10/US-202/College Hwy following hilly contours whereas the rail trail follows the railroad bed into the city crossing over the Westfield River heading up another 9 locks toward Lockhouse Road and Southampton.

Canal History: Canal opened between New Haven & Westfield in 1828. According to the book *Westfield and its Historic Influences*, Westfield celebrated its first cruise on December 9, 1829 (the canal boat *General Sheldon*, built in Westfield, arrived in Granby at midnight, the crew ate and with a short nap, arrived at Hillhouse's Basin in New Haven at ten-thirty in the morning). Canal boats plied the canal until 1848 when the railroad replaced canal travel (Operation of the canal between Westfield and Northampton was not open to navigation until late summer, 1835).

Civil Engineer, Jarvis Hurd, forecasted in 1826 that "The receipts into the treasury [i.e., the Hampshire & Hampden Canal Company] will be derived from the toll on all articles transported on the canal, and from the water power to be leased to individuals and to companies." The idea was that excess water from the Westfield River would feed the canal with water and this water would be a great source of water power for industry in northern Westfield onward to Easthampton. The feeder water came from a six mile canal starting "about half a mile above Salmon Falls, where a dam of eleven and one half feet will be required" in Woronoco, Massachusetts.

The village of Westfield gave engineers one of their biggest problems because Westfield was located in the hollow of a low point: The southern high point was on Congamond Lake in Southwick at 220 feet above sea level and the northern high point was in Westfield/Southampton at 232 feet above sea level. To solve this problem, the engineers built locks 1 to 9 dropping the water about seventy-eight feet north of Congamond Lake (Lock 9 is at the intersection of Shaker Road and Laro Road in Westfield). The canal stays at this level for about 6 miles, crossing Little River and Westfield River by aqueduct taking a sharp right after the river continuing until reaching lock 10 located just west of Lockhouse Road (between Arch Road and MA/90 overpass). Lock 10 followed by locks 11, 12 and 13 then 14, 15 and 16 raising a northbound boat some eighty feet. Then, a just little further, where Lockhouse Road crosses the railroad bed, locks 17 and 18 raise the boat another twenty feet or so reaching the summit toward Southampton. This high point was known as 'Timber Swamp Summit' because, as noted earlier, the summit is 232 feet above sea level (thus came the name 'Lockhouse Road'): [220′ – 78′ + 70′ + 20′ = 232′].

In the fall of 1831, a drought lowered the water in Congamond Lake to such an extent that traffic stopped for three months and subsequently a feeder line was constructed upstream from Westfield's Little River. At this same time, an intentional bad break in the canal occurred and "it was decided that all boats must be registered, and any having square corners must have these properly guarded; traffic rules were established, a boat going towards tide-water, or within 100 yards of, and at the same level as the water of, the lock that was approaching, had the right of way".

Without knowing it, as a youth, the author lived on or next to canal works: Once in Woronoco where the old feeder line went through what was called 'The Beehive' (project housing for paper mill workers) and as a teenager, when the canal paralleled houses along Westfield's Shaker Road near Little River.

Westfield's Little River Aqueduct was 300 feet long, six feet deep and 14 feet wide, supported by at least eight sandstone piers. A second much higher aqueduct in Westfield went over the Westfield River where the railroad/rail trail trestle is located. All remains of the Little River Aqueduct washed away long ago. Watercolor by Robert R Madison

Westfield South Basin or Port of Westfield, 1846 – Westfield Newsletter

CANAL RAILROAD

An old postcard showing the Railway Station in Westfield, MA dated SEP 25 1912. This picture shows the railroad tracks that parallel the Westfield River as the steam train heads west toward Albany, NY. The 'cow catcher' is just passing over the New York & New Haven tracks (which was the old canal - the railroad bridge over the river was called the 'Tin Bridge') with the Westfield River on the right next to the switching tower as the tracks head south toward New Haven, CT over the Westfield River.

Picture of a more modern Westfield Railway Station before the railroad bed was raised during the 'Great River Bridge Project.' In 2012, a revitalization project designed to improve the area (park, bridge, street and pedestrian areas) was conducted. As a student working his way through college at the nearby Fitzgerald Building Supply, the author remembers large trucks would get stuck trying to drive under this railroad bridge. Photo by Hoyt Willis - 1990.

Where's the railroad? In downtown Westfield, the elevated rail-trail follows the rail bed north toward the Westfield River and onward to Northampton. North of the Westfield River the railroad stays west of the on-street rail trail until both cross at the intersection of Lockhouse Rd and Turnpike Rd.

Railroad History: In 1856 the New Haven & Northampton RR (NH&N) was extended through Southwick into Westfield and ultimately to Northampton. The railroad bed was elevated on top of the old canal waterway (Canal Line) in downtown Westfield as it made its way toward the Westfield River to match the height of the Boston & Albany Railroad bed at the Westfield Depot on the east side of the Westfield River. In 1869 the old canal railway was operated by NY&NH and run by NHRR. The railroad was abandoned in 1976 and ultimately became the Southwick and Columbia Rail-Trail.

BICYCLE REPAIR AND RENTAL FACILITIES

New Horizons Sports, Inc.
55 Franklin St
Westfield, MA 01085
413 562-5237

OFF RAIL TRAIL EXCURSIONS

(Excursions may or may not require bicycles)

1. Westfield City Hall
59 Court St
Westfield, MA 01085
413 572-6200
www.cityofwestfield.org

2. Westfield Historical Commission
Westfield City Hall
59 Court St
Westfield, MA 01085
413 572-6200
www.cityofwestfield.org

Grandmother's Garden
(Smith Avenue next to Chauncey Allen Park and State Pool)

Amelia Park Ice Arena
(21 S Broad St)

Half Mile Falls Park
(Elm St/railroad underpass)

Stanley Park
(400 Western Ave)

Hampden Ponds State Park
(1048 North Rd)

Westfield Athenaeum Library
(6 Elm St)

RAIL TRAIL GUIDE

NORTH

HEADING SOUTH

MILES N		MILES S
7.9	⊗ **TRAILHEAD** @ Southampton, Brickyard Road	0
	↑ Brickyard becomes Root Rd.	0.3
	↑ Root Road becomes Lockhouse Rd.	2.4
	→ At the end of Lockhouse Rd take your right onto US-202/10/Elm St toward the Westfield River Bridge. NOTE: Bridges are 'one way'.	1.7
	↑ From the Westfield River Bridge, continue on Columbia Greenway Rail Trail toward Main St overpass (or downtown Elm St to Main St overpass and CGRT).	1.4
	↑ Continue on Columbia Greenway Rail Trail past Main Street overpass on CGRT to parking on Shaker Rd.	2.1
0.3	↑ Root Rd becomes Brickyard Rd at the border of Westfield and Southampton (at Valley Rd intersection).	
2.4	← Left onto Lockhouse Rd until arriving at Root Rd. NOTE: Busy traffic crossing to 'unclip' from US-202/MA-10/N Elm St to Lockhouse Rd. **Option** to continue on US-202/MA-10/N Elm St 0.3 mi. to ← left on Arch Rd to continue on Lockhouse Rd.	
1.7	↑ Westfield River Bridge/US-202/MA-10/N Elm St to Lockhouse Rd (traveling under railroad overpass).	
1.4	↑Main St to Westfield River Bridge & N Elm St.	
2.1	↑ Columbia Greenway Rail Trail (CGRT) parking on Shaker Rd to Main Street.	
0	⊗ **TRAILHEAD** @ Westfield, Shaker Road.	7.9

HEADING NORTH

SOUTH

SECTION 14: SOUTHAMPTON
(SOUTHAMPTON GREENWAY)

Common Name: East Coast Greenway, Southampton Greenway and Manhan Rail Trail

Route: Southampton Brickyard Rd to Easthampton Coleman Rd.

Total Distance: 6.4 miles or 30 – 45 minutes.

Ride Details: Skill level is moderate. Most bicycling is 'on street' (streets not heavily traveled). Elevation gain is moderately up and down.

Significant Canal Features: Nine locks (19 – 27) bring the canal level down nearly 90'. The masonry lock wall of Lock 22 still exists off College Highway (Brickyard Rd & MA-10/College Hwy).

Bicycling or hiking on Brickyard Road in Southampton, looking west, you will find railroad tracks in front of or behind residences. In this picture, the canal and railroad tracks follow one another. Along this route, Brickyard Road, the railroad and the canal crisscross each other until reaching MA-10/College Highway.

SOUTHAMPTON RAIL TRAIL MAP

SOUTHAMPTON GREENWAY

SOUTHAMPTON RAIL TRAIL

RAIL TRAIL:

NOTICE: Until Southampton's Greenway Rail Trail is complete, bikers can follow the suggested route or follow heavily traffic MA-10/College Hwy.

⊗**TRAILHEAD:** Southampton, MA. "On street" parking in the vicinity of Brickyard Rd/Valley Rd.

↑ Intersection of Brickyard Rd/Valley Rd head north on Brickyard Rd onto MA-10/College Highway 1.5 mi

← Left on MA-10/College Highway traveling a short distance.

→ Right onto Moose Brook Rd to Strong Rd 0.9 mi.

← Left onto Strong Rd to East St 0.9 mi.

→ Right onto East St onto Pleasant St 0.4 mi.

← Left onto Pleasant St 1.6 mi.

← Left onto Gunn Rd 0.1 mi.

→ Right onto Coleman Rd (at this point, Manhan Rail Trail begins) 0.9 mi.

NOTE: Current route is "on street" because the Southampton Greenway may be still under construction. When completed, follow the rail trail to the Manhan Rail Trail.

⊗**TRAILHEAD:** Southampton, MA. Parking on Coleman Rd near the entrance to Manhan Rail Trail.

DIRECTIONS SOUTH? Go to the Rail Trail Guide at the end of this chapter.

PARKING ACCESS:

Southampton, MA

• Trailhead GPS: 215 Brickyard Road ('on-street'), ZIP 01073.

• Parking at the intersection of Brickyard Rd and Valley Rd (quicker access from US-10/College Hwy along driving west along Valley Rd).

• Off street on intersection of Moose Brook Rd & US-10/College Hwy near Brickyard Rd intersection of US-10/ College Hwy (this is mid-trail).

• Mall parking at 10 College Hwy, Southampton, MA.

Easthampton, MA

• Trailhead GPS: 12 Coleman Road, ZIP 01027.

• On street parking on Coleman Rd, Manhan Rail Trail (MRT) where the Manhan Rail Trail begins.

SOUTHAMPTON HISTORY

Southampton is a rural farming and residential community nestled between low mountains and rolling hills. This was a frontier settlement with Indian raids a way of life (the land was purchased from the 'Non-o-tuck Indians'. Pioneers from Northampton came down and settled in the area called 'Newton-on-the-Manhan', a hilly area above the Manhan River. In 1753 the Town of Southampton was incorporated. Lumbering and forests cleared for farming were the significant items contributing to the prosperity of the community.

SOUTHAMPTON CANAL HISTORY

Where's the canal? From Westfield, the canal intertwines between the old railroad bed and 'on street' bikeways for most of the distance in Southampton until the intersection of MA-10/College Hwy and Brickyard Rd. At this point, the canal follows the old rail bed crossing over MA-10/ College Hwy just before Glendale Rd and the Easthampton border. Near this juncture on Coleman Rd, the proposed Southampton Greenway connects to the existing Manhan Rail Trail. The canal leaves the railroad bed just south of Gunn Road and does not return to the railroad bed or rail-trail until near the intersection of MA-10/Easthampton Road and Lovefield Street in Northampton.

Canal History: Canal water in the Southampton section of the canal comes from Salmon Falls, a natural waterfall in Woronoco's section of the Westfield River. As noted earlier, Jarvis Hurd, a Civil Engineer in 1826, was expecting 'water power' revenue from canal water. This Southampton high point was known as 'Timber Swamp Summit' because it is 232 feet above sea level (thus the name Lockhouse Road). The other high point to the south is 'Southwick Pond Summit' on Congamond Lake and this part of the canal is 220 feet above sea level.

Southampton had nine locks (19 – 27) dropping the water level down about 90' before leveling at Lock 27 at the Easthampton town line and into Northampton just before lock 28 near the Connecticut River. The masonry lock wall of Lock 22 still exists off College Highway (Brickyard Rd & MA-10/College Hwy). The bicyclist or passerby can still see the circa 1832 Lyman & Elder Storehouse on this corner (see picture next page). It took the lockkeeper about 5 minutes to fill up the lock with water so the canal boat could continue on its journey. The trip from Northampton to New Haven took about 24 hours. That's about 5 hours of locking and unlocking!

Circa 1832 Lyman & Elder Storehouse and Lock 22 Lockkeeper's house in Southampton, MA.. Watercolor by Robert R. Madison.

Of interest, when bicycling north along Brickyard Road, as you approach MA-10/College Highway, looking west in back of homes, you can still see the railroad bed that was once the old canal. Just before reaching College Highway, 4 Locks (19, 20, 21 and 22) bring the canal level down some 40′. As noted above, Lock 22 still exists off College Highway and it is an excellent example of how a masonry lock wall was constructed. A 60′ South Manhan River Aqueduct carried canal boats over the Manhan River (below Lock 22 east on College Highway- - just below the roadside mill and water dam) when the canal was in operation.

On the corner of Brickyard Road and MA-10/College Highway the winter remains of Lock 22 can be seen (2015 photo). A sign in front of the house reads "Hampshire and Hampden Canal, 1829 – 1847, Lock 22, East Wall, Original Lock Dimensions, 80'Long, 12' Wide, 7' Lift, Southampton Historical Commission".

CANAL RAILROAD

Charles Rufus Harte in 1933 took thousands of photographs of the canal system from New Haven to Northampton. This photo shows railroad tracks and Lock 22 in Southampton, MA.

Railroad bridge over the Manhan River (opposite the Lockmaster's House and the Lyman & Elder Storehouse). The Pioneer Valley Rail Road no longer utilizes this section of the railroad. Photograph taken in the Fall of 2015.

Where's the railroad? The railroad bed exists in most places, visible from on-street bicycling. In Southampton, they wind back and forth across the bikeway west of MA-10/College Hwy. The canal leaves the railroad bed just south of Gunn Road and does not return to the railroad bed or rail-trail until near the intersection of MA-10/Easthampton Rd. and Lovefield St. in Northampton.

Railroad History: In 1856 the New Haven & Northampton RR (NH&N) was extended through Southwick and ultimately to Northampton. The railroad lines were constructed in the canal bed from East Street south to the Westfield line. In 1869 the railroad was operated by NY&NH and run by NHRR. At one point the Pioneer Valley Rail Road operated part of the right-of-way. The railroad was abandoned in 1976 to become the Southampton Greenway Rail Trail.

BICYCLE REPAIR AND RENTAL FACILITIES

Southampton Bicycle
247 College Hwy
Southampton, MA 01073
413 538-7662

Custom Cycle Bike Shop
90 Cottage St
Easthampton, MA 01027

Fat Trax Snowboards
19 North St
Easthampton, MA 01027
413 586-8766

OFF RAIL TRAIL EXCURSIONS

(Excursions may or may not require bicycles)

1. Southampton Town Hall
210 College Highway
Southampton, MA 01073
413 527-8392
www.town.southampton.ma.us

2. Conant Memorial Park
(East St & Clark St)

3. Southampton Historical Commission
Edwards Public Library
30 East St
Southampton, MA 01073
413 527-9480

Pulaski Park
(191 College Hwy)

Edwards Public Library
(30 East St)

RAIL TRAIL GUIDE

NORTH

MILES N		HEADING SOUTH MILES S
6.4	⊗ **TRAILHEAD** @ Southampton, Coleman Road.	0
	↑ Coleman Rd at Manhan Rail Trail (near US-10/College Hwy) head south to Gunn Rd where you will turn left. [NOTE: ***It's possible to bike south 5.0 mi. on busy US-10/College Highway directly to Brickyard Rd***].	0.9
	← Left on Gunn Rd continue to Pleasant St.	0.1
	→Right onto Pleasant St to East St.	1.6
	→ Turn right onto East St traveling to Strong Rd.	0.4
	← Left onto Strong Rd.	0.9
	→ Right onto Moose Brook Rd coming to MA-10/ College Highway.	0.9
	← /→ Turn left on MA-10/College Highway a short distance then turn right Brickyard Rd to trailhead at the intersection of Brickyard Rd/Valley Rd.	1.6
0.9	→ Turn right onto Coleman Rd traveling to the Manhan Rail Trail junction.	
0.1	← Turn left onto Gunn Rd to Coleman Rd.	
1.6	← Turn left onto Pleasant St onto Gunn Rd.	
0.4	→ Turn right onto East St traveling to Pleasant St.	
0.9	← Turn left onto Strong Rd to East St.	
0.9	← /→ Turn left on MA-10/College Highway a short distance then turn right onto Moose Brook Rd. [NOTE: ***It's possible to bike north 5.0 mi. on busy US-10/College Highway directly to Coleman Rd and the Manhan Rail Trail***].	
1.6	↑ Parking along the sides of Brickyard Rd or Valley Rd head north on Brickyard Rd onto MA-10/College Highway.	
0	⊗ **TRAILHEAD** @ Southampton, Brickyard Road.	6.4
HEADING NORTH		

SOUTH

SECTION 15: EASTHAMPTON
(MANHAN RAIL TRAIL)

Common Names: East Coast Greenway, Bay State Greenway, Manhan Rail Trail and the Hampshire & Hampden Canal Rail Trail.

Route: Easthampton Coleman Rd to Northampton Ferry St along the Manhan Rail Trail just south of Northampton.

Total Distance: 2.7 miles or 15 – 20 minutes.

Ride Details: Skill level is easy, mostly flat & paved. Elevation gain is minimal. Restrooms available at Easthampton Public Safety Complex (32 Payson Ave) and seasonally at Millside Park (9 Ferry St).

Significant Canal Features: The Easthampton canal is level from border to border. The canal remains on the high side of the Manhan River as the river meanders on its way west of the Oxbow section of the Connecticut River.

Family outing on the Manhan Rail Trail and the 'New Haven – Northampton Canal Greenway', downtown Easthampton.

EASTHAMPTON RAIL TRAIL MAP

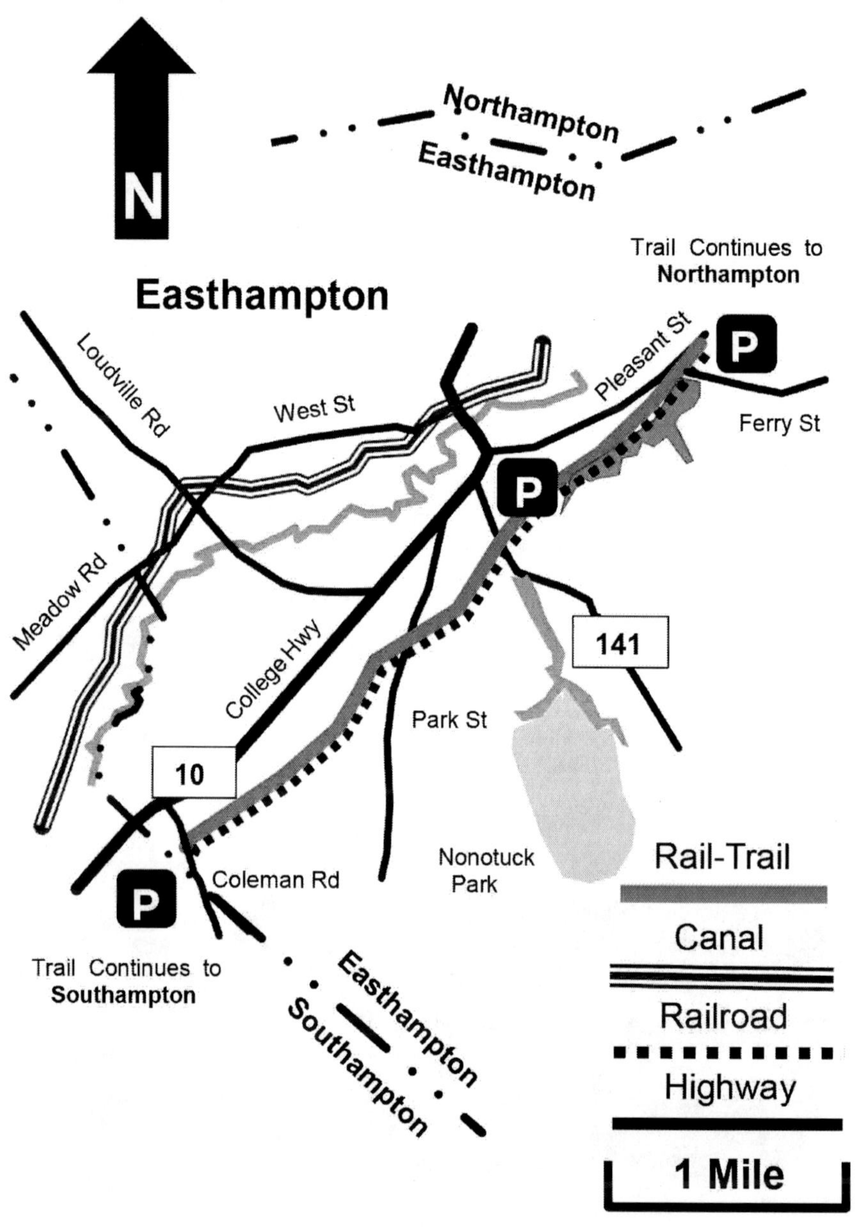

MANHAN RAIL TRAIL

EASTHAMPTON RAIL TRAIL

RAIL TRAIL:

⊗**TRAILHEAD:** Southampton, MA. Parking on Coleman Rd near the entrance to Manhan Rail Trail.

↑ Head north on Manhan Rail Trail (MRT) for 1.6 mi.

→ Short right on Payson St to Easthampton Public Safety Building returning to the MRT.

↑ Continue on MRT toward Northampton 1.1 mi.

⊗**TRAILHEAD:** Easthampton, MA. Parking at Lovefield St/Ferry St near the entrance to Manhan Rail Trail.

DIRECTIONS SOUTH? Go to the Rail Trail Guide at the end of this chapter.

PARKING ACCESS:

Easthampton MA

- Trailhead GPS: 12 Coleman Road, ZIP 01027.
- On street parking on Coleman Rd, Manhan Rail Trail (MRT) where trail begins.
- Street parking on intersection of South St and MRT.
- Trail access at Union St & Liberty St shopping areas and MRT.
- Parking at the Easthampton Public Safety Building at 32 Payson Ave, at Millside Park off of Ferry St.
- Ample parking in downtown Easthampton.

Easthampton MA (near Northampton, MA border)

- Trailhead GPS: 9 Ferry Street, ZIP 01027.

EASTHAMPTON HISTORY

Easthampton was settled in 1665. Prior to 1664, Easthampton was part of Northampton. As the settlement grew, areas around the Manhan River and around the Village of Pascommuck became popular areas to build homes and mill operations. Pascommuck is a Nipmuck Indian word describing 'where it bends' referring to the 'Ox-Bow' section of the Connecticut River. As late as 1809, Easthampton changed its charter and became the Town of Easthampton. In time, manufacturing became commonplace. The manufacture of buttons, elastics and rubber fabric as well as fabrics became popular because of water power.

EASTHAMPTON CANAL HISTORY

Where's the canal? The canal stays west of downtown Easthampton, US-10/South Main Street, the railroad bed and the Manhan River again crossing US-10 just northwest of Easthampton at the intersection of US-10/Northampton St and the Manhan River. The canal does not follow the railroad bed or rail-trail in Easthampton.

Canal History: According to Civil Engineer Jarvis Hurd, canal water reaching Easthampton comes from Salmon Falls, a natural waterfall in Woronoco's section of the Westfield River. Other tributaries into the Manhan River kept the canal full of water. Easthampton also shares the 60′ North Manhan River Aqueduct with Southampton. Aqueducts spanned very wide rivers. They were usually built in multiples of 40′ spans with diagonal reinforcing timbers supporting the heavy load. These 40′ spans rested on stone piers or abutments.

The spans trunks themselves were made of six 40′ 10″ x 12″ long chestnut timbers. The flume that carried water across the aqueduct was 14′ wide with 4′ of water to support canal boats. Many times, when horses were crossing aqueduct towpaths, they had to be blindfolded to prevent bolting. The canal itself was 36′ wide at the top with a depth of about 6′. The tow path where horses pulled barges or packet boats was 10′ wide and the opposite berm was about 7′ wide rising 2′ above the top of the water. The canal itself was built by hand. Trees, rocks and soil were removed by oxen, mule, and horse or by human muscles. When following hillsides, dirt was usually pulled from the high side to the low side to create both a 7′ berm and a towpath on the opposite side of the canal.

Horses pull a packet boat across a field as passengers sun themselves somewhere off West Street (the painting shows the packet boat after leaving Lock 27 then crossing the North Manhan River Aqueduct and crossing Loudville Road as it travels north to the Connecticut River). Mount Tom is in the background. Watercolor by Robert R. Madison.

This is one example of all that is left of the old Hampshire and Hampden Canal: this location is north of O'Neil Street. Looking closely at this picture, the viewer will see trash and debris left behind by careless people.

The author purposely choose this picture to emphasize that the main purpose of this rail trail book is to point out that many do not realize that an 'ancient' canal once connected Long Island Sound with the upper Connecticut River in Northampton. Over time, developers and careless people are destroying the canal. The purpose of the author's book is to collect funds so local historical societies can post 'NH &N CANAL CROSSING, 1828 – 1847' signage along its path. 1992 – Carl E. Walter photograph.

CANAL RAILROAD

Front view of Easthampton's Railroad Station.

Where's the railroad? The railroad bed exists in most places, visible from on-street bicycling. The bed stays east of MA-10/College Hwy through downtown Easthampton, crossing MA-141/Mountain Rd as it makes its way toward the Oxbow and the railroad parallel to the Connecticut River. The canal does not follow the railroad bed in Easthampton as it works its way to Northampton.

Photograph of a steam engine with passenger cars. Image is mounted on a plaque alongside the rail trail next to Easthampton's Railroad Station.

Railroad History: In 1856 the New Haven & Northampton RR (NH&N) was extended through Southwick and ultimately to Northampton. In 1869 the railroad was operated by NY&NH and run by NHRR. The Easthampton Station was built in 1914 over an older building. The railroad was abandoned in 1976 and became part of the Easthampton Rail-Trail.

BICYCLE REPAIR AND RENTAL FACILITIES

Custom Cycle Bike Shop
90 Cottage St
Easthampton, MA 01027

Fat Trax Snowboards
19 North St
Easthampton, MA 01027
413 586-8766

Southampton Bicycle
247 College Hwy
Southampton, MA 01073
413 538-7662

RAIL TRAIL EXCURSIONS

(Excursions may or may not require bicycles)

1. Easthampton Town Hall
50 Payson Ave
Easthampton, MA 01027
413 529-1460
www.easthampton.org

2. Nonotuck Park
(9 Daley Field Rd)

3. Easthampton Historical Society
200 Maine St
Easthampton, MA 01027
www.historicaleasthampton.com

Millside Park & Flaherty Park
(2 Ferry St)

Katherine Root Wayside Park
(US-10/Florence Rd)

Pulaski Park
(191 College Hwy)

Emily Memorial Library
(9 Park St)

RAIL TRAIL GUIDE

NORTH

MILES N		HEADING SOUTH MILES S
2.7	⊗ **TRAILHEAD** @ Southampton, Ferry Street.	0
	↑ Ferry St onto Manhan Rail Trail traveling south (optional stop on Payson St).	1.1
	↑ Continue back onto Manhan Rail Trail to Coleman Road.	1.6
1.1	↑ Continue back onto Manhan Rail Trail to Ferry Street.	
1.6	↑ Coleman Rd onto Manhan Rail Trail traveling north traveling (optional stop on Payson St).	
0	⊗ **TRAILHEAD** @ Southampton, Coleman.Road	2.7
HEADING NORTH		

SOUTH

SECTION 16: NORTHAMPTON
(MANHAN RAIL TRAIL AND THE NEW HAVEN AND NORTHAMPTON CANAL RAIL TRAIL)

Common Names: East Coast Greenway, Northampton Bike Path, Manhan Rail Trail, Northampton Bikeway, Norwottuck Bike Trail and the New Haven & Northampton Canal Rail Trail.

Route: Northampton Ferry St to Northampton Damon Rd.

Total Distance: 6.0 miles or 30 – 45 minutes.

Ride Details: On Manhan Rail Trail: Skill level is easy. Elevation gain is minimal. Mix of rail trail and busy city streets.

'On Street' Canal Route: Skill level is easy. Elevation gain is minimal. Ride is flat in town. Mostly on busy city streets. Care should be taken. Significant Canal Features: Locks 28 – 32, the last 5 locks of the canal system, from New Haven to the Connecticut River in Northampton, are no longer visible. All remnants of the canal are almost long gone. One can still be able to find the canal entrance or cut just above Elwell Island on the Northampton side of the river (see canal history picture).

Rail trail bridge over the Connecticut River near the Connecticut River Greenway Park in Northampton, MA.

NORTHAMPTON RAIL TRAIL MAP

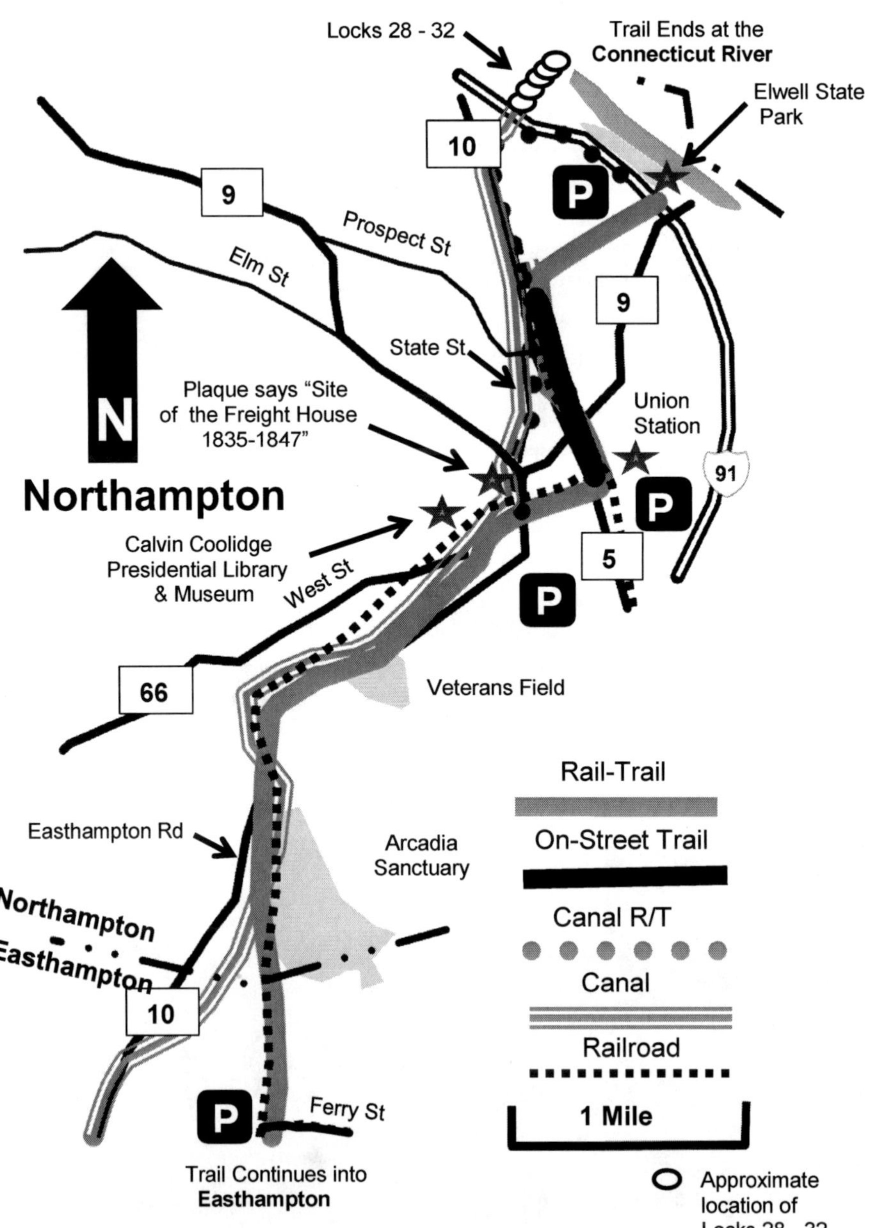

MANHAN RAIL TRAIL AND CANAL ROUTE

NORTHAMPTON RAIL TRAIL

RAIL TRAIL:

'Manhan Rail Trail' route toward CT River

⊗**TRAILHEAD:** Easthampton, MA. Parking off Ferry St near the entrance to Manhan Rail Trail.

← Right onto the Manhan Rail Trail (MRT) 0.3 mi.

← Slight turn on MRT (NOTE JUNCTION: right to Northampton, left toward the Oxbow south of the city of Northampton.

↑ Continue north following MRT 1.8 mi.

← Slight left onto Earle St

→ Right on MRT 0.9 mi.

← Left onto Old S St 0.1 mi.

→ Right onto MRT 0.9 mi.

← Slight left onto Pleasant St

→ Right onto Norwottuck Rail Trail 0.2 mi.

← Short left (after Route 9 bridge overpass) narrow bike path leads to Merrick Ln, left toward Main St. and Route 9 0.1 mi.

(NOTE: Traveling further and crossing railroad tracks is dangerous. Several 'off trail' dirt paths exist near the King Street and Norwottuck Rail Trail intersection. Posted rail trail signs direct the hiker or biker along published routes).

← Slight left onto Main St. traveling under railroad overpass.

← Left onto Market St 0.3 mi.

↑ Market St. becomes North St 0.2 mi.

← Left onto Woodmont Rd. 0.2 mi.

→ Right onto Norwottuck Rail Trail, 0.7 mi.

⊗**TRAILHEAD:** Northampton, MA. Parking at the Connecticut River Greenway Park on Damon Rd.

RAIL TRAIL:

'Canal' route toward CT River

⊗**TRAILHEAD:** Easthampton, MA. Parking off Ferry St near the entrance to Manhan Rail Trail.

← Right onto the Manhan Rail Trail (MRT) 0.3 mi.

← Slight right on MRT (NOTE JUNCTION: right to Northampton, left toward the Oxbow south of the city of Northampton).

↑ Continue north following MRT 1.8 mi.

← Left on intersection of MRT/Grove St/East St continuing on MRT 0.6 mi.

← Leave MRT onto left at West St

→ Right onto West St/MA-66 0.3 mi.

← Right onto and crossing Elm St/Main St 0.1 mi.

(NOTE: State St route deviates from published Northampton Bike Path or Manhan Rail Trail because the NH&N Canal was on State St. Bikers can also follow this Manhan Rail Trail or Northampton Bike Path and arrive at the Connecticut River Greenway Park on Damon Rd).

← Left onto State St 0.7 mi.

→ Right onto Church St 0.1 mi.

← Left onto King St/Route 5 0.7 mi.

(NOTE: Traveling a few feet and heading east, the biker or hiker will connect to the 11 mile Norwottuck Rail Trail linking to Hadley and Amherst, or, one can continue 0.7 miles to Damon Rd. following closely the canal route. This route crosses busy Route 5 and over railroad tracks. Or, traveling a few feet and heading west, the biker or hiker will connect to the Northampton Bikeway heading toward Florence, MA.).

→ Right on Damon Rd 0.5 mi.

(NOTE: Traveling under highway US-91, on your left, locks 28 – 32 lowered the New Haven & Northampton Canal to the level of the Connecticut River. This is the effective end of the trail! Parking exists off street or the Connecticut River Greenway Park).

⊗**TRAILHEAD:** Northampton, MA

Parking at the Connecticut River Greenway Park on Damon Rd.

PARKING ACCESS:

Easthampton MA (near Northampton border)

- Trailhead GPS: 9 Ferry Street ZIP 01027.

- Parking at the Easthampton Public Safety Building at 32 Payson Ave, at Millside Park off of Ferry St.

- Ample parking in downtown Easthampton.

- Street parking on intersection of South St and MRT.

- Trail access at Union St & Liberty St shopping areas and MRT.

- On street parking on Coleman Rd Manhan Rail Trail (MRT) where trail begins.

Northampton MA

- Trailhead GPS: 136 Damon Road, ZIP 01060.

- Parking on Damon Rd Connecticut River Greenway State Park, 136 Damon Rd, Northampton, MA (right off US-91, Exit 19). Restrooms available.

- Parking off Lovefield St/Ferry St. Lovefield St is located off US-10/ Northampton St and US-91 (take Exit 18 driving south on US-5/Mt. Tom Rd to taking a right on East St then a right on Fort Hill Rd and a left on Clapp St to a right on Lovefield St).

- Parking at Veterans Field off MRT south of downtown Northampton.

- On street parking at intersection of MRT overpass and US-10.

- Nearby Arcadia Wildlife Sanctuary on Combs Rd off Fort Hill Rd.

- Multiple free and paid parking throughout the Northampton area.

- Metered parking off Railroad Ave.

- Paid parking at Look Park and limited off street parking nearby.

DIRECTIONS SOUTH? Go to the Rail Trail Guide at the end of this chapter.

NORTHAMPTON HISTORY

Northampton is made up of outer villages of Florence and Leeds. The city was settled in 1653 and incorporated in 1884. The founders were Puritan in nature and found the area around the Connecticut River to be fruitful and the Indians willing to trade. The settlers petitioned the General Court to "plant, possess and inhabit Nonotuck." The King Phillip War of 1675, spearheaded by Chief Metacomet, was a major issue with the settlers of that era. Northampton is another typical New England community that maintains a historic nature. A trip downtown helps the visitor to appreciate what the architecture of an earlier era looked like. Industries in this community were owned and operated by a silk mill. Education became a staple of Northampton over the years.

NORTHAMPTON CANAL HISTORY

Where's the canal? The canal crosses Lovefield St very close to the US-10/ Easthampton Rd intersection; following the rail bed north and re-crosses US-10/Easthampton Rd near Mill River and South Park Terrace following the contours of the land between West St and South St crossing Main St straight up State St onto Damon Rd/US-91/Boston & Maine Railroad tracks to the Connecticut River.

Canal History: Northampton was the northern most connection of the canal that extended all the way to New Haven and the oceans of the world. Construction began in Connecticut in 1822 and the canal was started in Northampton in late 1826. The success of the railroad in 1845 led to the final closing of the canal in 1847.

The Honorable James Hillhouse reported in 1827 that the basin in Northampton will be the crossroads of goods and traffic moving down from the "rich country to the north, even Canada" to Boston or down the river to Hartford or to New Haven via the canal. A Northampton Hampshire Gazette article exclaimed "We take great satisfaction in extending the tidings, that there is now water communication between Northampton and New Haven. The first boat arrived from Westfield on the 4th." It was further reported "when suddenly about 4 o'clock, sounds arose totally inconsistent with the quiet of the day. Bells rung, the cannon pealed, and there was a general rush for the canal. A boat hove in sight, drawn by four grey horses, enlivened with a band of music, and was greeted with a profound huzza from the collected crowd". In 1836 the Farmington Canal Company and the Hampshire and Hampden Company of Massachusetts became the New Haven and Northampton Canal Company.

After unloading passengers in downtown Northampton, the canal boat finally reaches the Connecticut River Basin. Watercolor by Robert R. Madison.

Canal water came all the way from Salmon Falls, a natural waterfall in Woronoco's section of the Westfield River, slowly, along with other water sources, worked its way south and north to Northampton and ultimately the Connecticut River in Northampton, Massachusetts.

A plaque was placed at the corner of East Street and Main Street to commemorate that the canal passed this way. The plaque simply says *"Site of the Freight House. 1835 – 1847. Northampton – New Haven Canal. This canal passed under Main Street through a stone archway, thence up State Street ending at the 'Honey Pot' on the Connecticut River. The Northampton Historical Society. 1941".*

Lock 32 on the west side of the Connecticut River. Unseen on the left side of this photograph would be a wharf used by canal boats to load or offload commerce. To the right is where the canal entered the Connecticut River. The goal was to someday continue the canal all the way to the Saint Lawrence River in Canada.

CANAL RAILROAD

Where's the railroad? The rail bed and the Manhan Rail Trail or Northampton Bike Path is mostly the same if you follow the posted rail trail signs toward the Union Station traveling north. NOTE: The second 'canal' route toward the CT River described above tries to follow the original canal route, not the railroad route north of Main Street.

Railroad History: In 1856 the New Haven & Northampton RR (NH&N) was extended through Southwick and ultimately to Northampton. In 1869 the railroad was operated by NY&NH and run by NHRR. The railroad was abandoned in 1976 to become the Northampton Rail Trail. (The Connecticut River Railroad was formed in 1845 when the Northampton and Springfield Railroad merged with the Greenfield and Northampton Railroad. These railroads were acquired by the Boston and Maine Railroad (B&M). The B&M Railroad Bridge over the Connecticut River is now a connector to the Norwottuck & Massachusetts Central Rail Trail).

Union Station in Northampton, MA (looking south) was built in 1896. Just north of here the original Connecticut River Rail Road Station and the New Haven & Northampton Railroad Station pictured on the next page existed before they were torn down (near Strong Ave and Main St) and replaced by the Union Station. The Norwottuck Bike Trail passes on the other side of the Union Station.

The image on the left is the Connecticut River Depot, the middle image is the New Haven & Northampton Depot and on the right is the Union Station as they existed in the later part of the 19th Century.

BICYCLE REPAIR AND RENTAL FACILITIES

Northampton Bicycle
319 Pleasant St
Northampton, MA 01060
413 586-3810
http://www.nohobike.com/

Mountain Goat
189 Main St
Northampton, MA 01060
413 586-0803

Full Circle Bike Shop
46 Maple St
Florence, MA 01062
413 585-8700

OFF RAIL TRAIL EXCURSIONS

(Excursions may or may not require bicycles)

1. Northampton City Hall
210 Main St
Northampton, MA 01060
413 587-1249
www.northamptonma.gov

2. Northampton has excellent bike trails that can be reached from the canal rail-trail. The first is the Northampton Bike Path, about 2 miles west from US-5/King St leading to the 150 acre Look Memorial Park. Known as Look Park, the park has restrooms, picnic tables, a playground and other activities. The second bike trail, the Norwottuck Bike Trail is east of US-5/King St heading about 8 miles across the Connecticut River to Amherst.

3. Historic Northampton Museum & Education Center
46 Bridge St
Northampton, MA 01060
413 584-6011
www.historic-northampton. org

Connecticut River Greenway State Park
(Damon Rd)

Childs Park
(North Elm & Woodlawn Ave)

Look Park
(300 North Main St, Florence)

Calvin Coolidge Presidential Library & Museum and Forbes Library
(20 West St)

NOTES

SOURCE NOTES

From a research standpoint, the author is limited to the number of sources in print. Except where I have bushwhacked through woods and tromped back and forth along steams to locate towpaths and locks, my sources are limited to reprints of public records whereas others come directly from local experts in town or city historical societies. Still others come directly from the research writings of those who have spent a greater part of their lives documenting the New Haven & Northampton notably Carl E. Walter, Arthur W. Sweeton, Ruth S. Hummel, Charles R. Harte and others. I decided not to rewrite the works of those to whom I do not hold a historical candle to; rather, I believe I can best describe their life's work by quoting from their works and documenting sources of material.

Below you will find, by chapter, the list the books, websites, archived works, public records, newspaper articles quotations from local experts that constitute the main sources for this book.

PROFILE OF ELEVATIONS

- Google Earth; MAPQUEST; NOAA; Maps, books or lectures by Ruth S. Hummel and Carl E. Walter.

BIKE SAFETY, RULES AND REGULATIONS

- Massachusetts General Laws, Chapter 85, Section 11B
- The League of American Bicyclists
- The International Mountain Bike Association

SECTION 1: NEW HAVEN

• Comments on New Haven's history taken from New Haven's website www.cityofnewhaven.com/

• Some canal descriptions and each lock location from 2000 Map of the Farmington Canal by Ruth Sharp Hummel and Carl E. Walter.

• Turner, M. Gregg and Jacobus, Melancthon, Connecticut Railroads ...An Illustrated History. (Manchester, CT: Allied Printing Services. 1989.) A publication by The Connecticut Historical Society.

•http://www.cityofnewhaven.com/Mayor/History_New_Haven.asp. A short history of New Haven.

• Karr, Ronald Dale, Lost Railroads of New England. (Pepperell, MA: Branch Line Press. 1989.)

•http://www.traillink.com/trail-reviews/farmington-canal-heritage-trail-.aspx

•http://magic.lib.uconn.edu/mash_up/nynhhrr_index.html. Railroad and canal right-of-way valuation maps by UCONN University Libraries.

• Farmington Canal Rail to Trail Association. www.farmingtoncanal.org.

• Harte, Charles Rufus, Connecticut Canals. (CT Society of Engineers. 1939.)

• Farmington Valley Greenway. www.fvgreenway.org.

• East Coast Greenway. www.greenway.org.

• Old canal bed photos. www.pdfhoStfocus.nps.gov/docs/NRHP/Photos/ 85002664.pdf

PHOTOGRAPH CREDITS:

The Farmington Canal Greenway signpost in New Haven, 2015 – Robert R. Madison

Canal boat PIONEER off Grand Avenue in New Haven. – New Haven Colonial Historical Society

Railroad tracks next to the Farmington Canal Heritage Trail near the Yale Campus in New Haven, 2015 – Robert R. Madison

SECTION 2: HAMDEN

• Hamden, CT webpage: www.hamden.com.

• Comments on Hamden's history taken from Hamden's website www.hamdenct.org.

• Some canal descriptions and each lock location from 2000 Map of the Farmington Canal by Ruth Sharp Hummel and Carl E. Walter.

• Harte, Charles Rufus, Connecticut Canals. (CT Society of Engineers. 1939.)

•http://magic.lib.uconn.edu/mash_up/nynhhrr_index.html. Railroad and canal right-of-way valuation maps by UCONN University Libraries.

• Farmington Canal Rail to Trail Association. www.farmingtoncanal.org.

• Farmington Valley Greenway. www.fvgreenway.org.

• Farmington Canal Trail. www.farmingtoncanal.org.

• East Coast Greenway. www.greenway.org.

PHOTOGRAPH CREDITS:

Bicyclist on the canal towpath near Lock 14, 2015 – Robert R. Madison

Lock 14 and the lockkeeper's house in the background, 2015 – Robert R. Madison

New Haven & Northampton Railroad Canal Line sign, 2015 – Robert R. Madison

SECTION 3: CHESHIRE

- Comments on Cheshire's history taken from Cheshire's website: http://www.cheshirect.org/ and www.connecticuthistory.org/towns-page/Chesire

- Harte, Charles Rufus, Connecticut Canals. (CT Society of Engineers. 1939.)

- Some canal descriptions and each lock location from 2000 Map of the Farmington Canal by Ruth Sharp Hummel and Carl E. Walter.

- The Cheshire Historical Society & Raimon L. Beard, Reflections on the Canal in Cheshire. (The Cheshire Historical Society, Inc., Cheshire, Connecticut. 1976.)

- Karr, Ronald Dale, Lost Railroads of New England. (Pepperell, MA: Branch Line Press. 1989.)

PHOTOGRAPH CREDITS:

Cheshire rail trail in earl fall, 2015 – Robert R. Madison

Lock 12, Farmington Canal Linear Park, 2015 – Robert R. Madison

Railroad arch in the Farmington Canal Linear Park, 2015 – Robert R. Madison

SECTION 4: SOUTHINGTON

• Comments on Southington's history taken from Southington's website: http://www.southington.org/content/17218/default.aspx.

• Some canal descriptions and each lock location from 2000 Map of the Farmington Canal by Ruth Sharp Hummel and Carl E. Walter.

• Harte, Charles Rufus, Connecticut Canals. (CT Society of Engineers. 1939. Includes quotations from Annual Report, Conn. Soc. C.E.1933.) Wiley, "Early Cement etc." and quotations from "An Ericsson Propeller on the Farmington Canal," *The Connecticut Magazine*, Vol. VII, Page 329.

• Karr, Ronald Dale, Lost Railroads of New England. (Pepperell, MA: Branch Line Press. 1989.)

• Southington Historical Society website: www.southingtonhistory.homestead.com/AbouttheSouthingtonHistoricalSociety.html

PHOTOGRAPH CREDITS:

Strolling along Southington's Rails-to-Trails Greenway, 2015 – Robert R. Madison

Canal's 'Long Level', 2015 – Robert R. Madison

Milldale Railroad Depot, 2015 – Robert R. Madison

SECTION 5: PLAINVILLE

• Comments on Plainville's history taken from Plainville's website: http://www.plainvillect.com/pages/page_content/Plainville_home.aspx and Plainville CT historical site: www.plainvillehistory.org

• Some canal descriptions from 2000 Map of the Farmington Canal by Ruth Sharp Hummel and Carl E. Walter.

• Harte, Charles Rufus, Connecticut Canals. (CT Society of Engineers. 1939.)

• Roy, John H. Jr., A Field Guide to Southern New England Railroad Depots and Freight Houses. (Pepperell, MA: Branch Line Press. 2007.)

• Castle, Henry Allen, The History of Plainville, Connecticut, 1640 – 1918. (Published by the Plainville Historical Society. 1966.)

• www.connecticuthistory.org/towns-page/plainville/

• Karr, Ronald Dale, Lost Railroads of New England. (Pepperell, MA: Branch Line Press. 1989.)

• Hummel, Ruth S., The Farmington Canal in Plainville Connecticut. (Printed by Briarwood Printing Co., Inc. 2007.)

PHOTOGRAPH CREDITS:

Photograph of the East Main Street Plainville Bicycle Travelway, 2015 – Robert R. Madison

Raymond Holden watercolor painting – Canton Historical Society

Canal Line Railroad: Author took the liberty to put a picture of a 1800's steam locomotive into a recent photograph of railroad tracks about to cross Broad Street in Plainville, 2015 – Robert R. Madison

SECTION 6: FARMINGTON

• Comments on Farmington's history taken from Farmington's website: http://www.farmington-ct.org/

• Some canal descriptions from 2000 Map of the Farmington Canal by Ruth Sharp Hummel and Carl E. Walter.

• Charles Rufus Harte, Some Engineering Features of the Old Northampton Canal. (Connecticut Society of Civil Engineers. 1933.)

• http://www.fvgreenway.org/map/maps.asp?id=1

• Harte, Charles Rufus, Connecticut Canals. (CT Society of Engineers. 1939)

• Some canal descriptions from 2006 Map of the Hampshire & Hampden Canal by Carl E. Walter.

PHOTOGRAPH CREDITS:

Bicyclists on the Farmington Canal Heritage Trail, 2015 – Robert R. Madison

1869 photograph by Karl Klauser of the Farmington Aqueduct - Farmington Historical Society

Farmington Railroad Station on Depot Street, 2015 – Robert R. Madison

SECTION 7: AVON

• Comments on Avon's history taken from Avon's website: http://www.town.avon.ct.us/

• Avon canal quote taken from the Avon Historical Society's website.
• Avon Farmington Valley Greenway website: http://www.fvgreenway .org/map/maps.

• Avon Historical Society: www.avonhistoricalsociety.org/FarmingtonCanal.

•Roy, John H. Jr., A Field Guide to Southern New England Railroad Depots and Freight Houses. (Pepperell, MA: Branch Line Press. 2007.)

•Karr, Ronald Dale, Lost Railroads of New England. (Pepperell, MA: Branch Line Press. 1989.)

•Some canal descriptions from 2006 Map of the Hampshire & Hampden Canal by Carl E. Walter.

PHOTOGRAPH CREDITS:

Rail Trail in Avon, 2015 – Robert R. Madison

Avon Historical Society marker on Rt 44 2015 – Robert R. Madison

Railroad overpass on Arch Road, 2015 – Robert R. Madison

SECTION 8: SIMSBURY

• Historical quote of Simsbury taken directly from Town of Simsbury's web page.: www.simsbury-ct.gov/.

• Simsbury Historical Society, 800 Hopmeadow St, Simsbury, CT 06070. 860-658-2500. http://simsburyhistory.org/

• Harte, Charles Rufus, Connecticut Canals. (CT Society of Engineers. 1939.)

• Some canal descriptions from 2000 Map of the Farmington Canal by Ruth Sharp Hummel and Carl E. Walter.

• Other canal descriptions came from historical works such as Ruth S. Hummel's The Farmington Canal in Plainville Connecticut. (Briarwood Printing Company. 2007.)

• Karr, Ronald Dale, Lost Railroads of New England. (Pepperell, MA: Branch Line Press. 1989.)

PHOTOGRAPH CREDITS:

Bicyclists on the Farmington Rail Trail, 2015 – Robert R. Madison

Author on Simsbury's Old Canal Way, 2015 – Robert R. Madison

Simsbury Railroad Depot on Railroad Street, 2015 – Robert R. Madison

SECTION 9: EAST GRANBY

• Comments on East Granby's history taken from East Granby's website. www.eastgranbyct.org/

• East Granby Historical Society, 24 Center St, East Granby, CT 06026. 860-653-3002. www.eastgranby.com/historicalsociety/.

• Some canal descriptions from 2000 Map of the Farmington Canal by Ruth Sharp Hummel and Carl E. Walter.

• Refer to Lake Basile Association for events. www.LakeBasile.org/

• Harte, Charles Rufus, Connecticut Canals. (CT Society of Engineers. 1939.)

• www.history.rays-place.com/ct/east-granby.htm

• Karr, Ronald Dale, Lost Railroads of New England. (Pepperell, MA: Branch Line Press. 1989.)

PHOTOGRAPH CREDITS:

Rail Trail near Lake Basile, 2015 – Robert R. Madison
Lake Basile next to the Farmington Canal, 2015 – Robert R. Madison

Granby Station, 2015 – Robert R. Madison

SECTION 10: GRANBY

• Comments on Granby's history taken from Granby's website. www.granby-ct.gov.

• Some canal descriptions and each lock location from 2000 Map of the Farmington Canal by Ruth Sharp Hummel and Carl E. Walter.

• Beard, Raimon, Reflections On The Canal In Cheshire. (The Cheshire Historical Society, Inc. June 1976.) Includes article on page 20 by Brown, E.R. "The Old Farmington Canal" *The Cheshire-Hamden Times*, March 15, 1923.

• Turner, M. Gregg and Jacobus, Melancthon, Connecticut Railroads ...An Illustrated History. (Manchester, CT: Allied Printing Services. 1986.) A publication by The Connecticut Historical Society. 1989.

PHOTOGRAPH CREDITS:

Canal Greenway in Granby, 2015 – Robert R. Madison

Salmon Brook Arch, 1933 – Charles Rufus Harte

Railroad Trestle over Salmon Brook, 2015 – Robert R. Madison

SECTION 11: SUFFIELD

• Comments on Suffield's history taken from Suffield's website: http://www.suffieldtownhall.com/

• Some canal descriptions from 2000 Map of the Farmington Canal by Ruth Sharp Hummel and Carl E. Walter.

• Suffield Historical Society, 232 Main St, Suffield, CT 06078. 860-668-5256. http://www. suffieldhistoricalsociety.org/

• Harte, Charles Rufus, Connecticut Canals. (CT Society of Engineers. 1939.)

• Karr, Ronald Dale, Lost Railroads of New England. (Pepperell, MA: Branch Line Press. 1989.)

PHOTOGRAPH CREDITS:

State rail trail marker between Connecticut and Massachusetts, 2015 – Robert R. Madison

Author and lecturer Carl E. Walter, 2013 – Robert R. Madison

Rail trail overpass over original NH&N railroad abutments on Phelps Rd in West Suffield, 2015 – Robert R. Madison

SECTION 12: SOUTHWICK

• "Jog" historical quote on Southwick taken directly from Town of Southwick's web page: http://www.southwickma.org/public_ documents/index

• Harte, Charles Rufus, Connecticut Canals. (CT Society of Engineers. 1939.)

• Some canal descriptions and each lock location from 2006 Map of the Hampshire & Hampden Canal by Carl E. Walter.

• Southwick Historical Society, Inc., 86 College Hwy., Southwick, MA 01077. 413-569-0436. http://www.southwickhistoricalsociety.org/.

• Hurd, Jarvis, Executive Committee Report of the Hampshire and Hampden Canal Corp., (April 3, 1826.) See bibliography

• Friends of the Southwick Rail Trail: www.southwick railtrail.org.

• Southwick Bicentennial Committee, Southwick Massachusetts 1770 – 1970 Bicentennial, 1969.

• Karr, Ronald Dale, Lost Railroads of New England. (Pepperell, MA: Branch Line Press. 1989.)

• Turner, Gregg M & Jacobus, Melancthon W., Connecticut Railroads an Illustrated History, (Connecticut Historical Society, 1989.)

PHOTOGRAPH CREDITS:

Bicyclist on the rail trail south of Congamond Lake, 2015 – Robert R. Madison

Canal entrance/exit just south of Congamond's South Pond, 2015 – Robert R. Madison

Southwick Depot and Congamond Depot - Southwick Historical Society

SECTION 13: WESTFIELD

• Comments on Westfield's history taken from Westfield's TBD's website: www.cityofwestfield.org/.
• Hurd, Jarvis, Executive Committee Report of the Hampshire and Hampden Canal Corp., (by Thomas Shepard on April 3, 1826. See bibliography.

• Harte, Charles Rufus, Connecticut Canals. (CT Society of Engineers. 1939.)

• Some canal descriptions and each lock location from 2006 Map of the Hampshire & Hampden Canal by Carl E. Walter.

• Western Hampden Historical Society, 87 South Maple St, Westfield, MA 01085 413-562-0612. http://www.thedeweyhouse.org/

• Unknown author, Westfield and its Historic Influences.

• Karr, Ronald Dale, Lost Railroads of New England. (Pepperell, MA: Branch Line Press. 1989.)

• Friends of the Columbia Greenway Rail Trail. www.columbiagreenway.org.

PHOTOGRAPH CREDITS:

Rail trail and NH&N Canal connects, 2015 – Robert R. Madison

Port of Westfield – Westfield Newsletter

Westfield Depot, then & now, 2015 – Hoyt Willis

SECTION 14: SOUTHAMPTON

• Comments on Southampton's history taken from Southampton's website: www.town.southampton.ma.us/.

• Some canal descriptions and each lock location from 2006 Map of the Hampshire & Hampden Canal by Carl E. Walter.

• Hurd, Jarvis, Executive Committee Report of the Hampshire and Hampden Canal Corp., (by Thomas Shepard on April 3, 1826.) See bibliography.

• Congregational Church website: www.shcong.org/about/history

• Southampton Greenway Committee. www.southamptongreenway.org.

PHOTOGRAPH CREDITS:

On Street biking on Brickyard Road, 2015 – Robert R. Madison

Remains of Lock 22 on College Highway, 2015 – Robert R. Madison

Charles Rufus Harte 1933 photo of Lock 22.

On-street railroad tracks, 2015 – Robert R. Madison

SECTION 15: EASTHAMPTON

• Comments on Easthampton's history taken from Easthampton's website: http://www.easthamptonweb.com/ourcommunity/pages/history.html

• Some canal descriptions and each lock location from 2006 Map of the Hampshire & Hampden Canal by Carl E. Walter.

• Easthampton Historical Society, 7 Holyoke St, Easthampton, MA 01027. 413-527-3108.

• Hurd, Jarvis. Executive Committee Report of the Hampshire and Hampden Canal Corp., April 3, 1826. See bibliography.

• Friends of the Manhan Rail Trail. www.manhanrailtrail.org.

PHOTOGRAPH CREDITS:

Manhan Rail Trail. Family outing on the Manhan Rail Trail and the 'New Haven – Northampton Canal', 2015 – Robert R. Madison

NH&N Canal. Canal North of O'Neil Street, 1992 – Carl E. Walter

Canal Railroad. Front view of Easthampton's Railroad Station, 2015 – Robert R. Madison

SECTION 16: NORTHAMPTON

- Comments on Northampton's history taken from Northampton's website: www.northamptonma.gov/aboutNorthampton/History_of_Northampton/

- Northampton City website: www.northamptonma.gov/.

- Hillhouse, Hon. James, H&H Canal Extension. 1827. See Bibliography.

- Forbes Library, 20 West St, Northampton, MA 01060. 413-527-3108. Historic Northampton website: www.historic-northampton.org/.

- Hurd, Jarvis, Executive Committee Report of the Hampshire and Hampden Canal Corp., (by Thomas Shepard on April 3, 1826.) See bibliography.

- One of many web sources: www.bikeitorhikeit.org/.

- Some canal descriptions and each lock location from 2006 Map of the Hampshire & Hampden Canal by Carl E. Walter.

- Daily Hampshire Gazette Newspaper. Canal Navigable. July 15, 1935.

- Karr, Ronald Dale, Lost Railroads of New England. (Pepperell, MA: Branch Line Press. 1989.)

- Friends of Northampton Trails and Greenways. www.fntg.net.

PHOTOGRAPH CREDITS

Norwottuck Bike Trail over the Connecticut River, 2015 – Robert R. Madison

NH&N Canal entrance & exit to the Connecticut River, 2015 – Robert R. Madison

Union Station in Northampton, 2015 – Robert R. Madison

Connecticut River Depot, New Haven & Northampton Depot and the Union Station - Wikipedia

FOLLOW THE NEW HAVEN AND NORTHAMPTON CANAL GREENWAY BIKE AND RAIL TRAILS

SELECTED BIBLIOGRAPHY

CANALS – BOOKS

Beard, Raimon L., Reflections On The Canal In Cheshire. (The Cheshire Historical Society, Inc., Cheshire, CT. June, 1976.)

Hummel, Ruth S., The Farmington Canal In Plainville Connecticut, (Plainville Historical Society, Inc. 2007)

Gay, Julius, The Farmington Canal. (Hartford: Case, Lockwood and Brainerd, 1929. Reprinted by the Plainville Historical Society, 1994.)

CANALS – PERIODICALS

THE HISTORY OF THE CANAL SYSTEM BETWEEN NEW HAVEN AND NORTHAMPTON. Camposeo, James Mark. 1822-1849. *Historical Journal of Western Massachusetts,* Fall, 1977

TRIO AND TRIPOD: IN THE TUNXIS VALLEY. Carrington, George H. *Connecticut Quarterly.* Jan-Mar, 1985 1:21-32

HAMPSHIRE & HAMPDEN CANAL COMPANY REPORTS

REPORT OF JARVIS HURD, ESQ, HAMPSHIRE AND HAMPDEN CANAL COMPANY. Jarvis Hurd, Esq., Civil Engineer. A report with an estimate of expense to complete the canal from the termination of the Farmington Canal, on the line of the Town of Southwick, to the great bend of Connecticut River at Northampton. 1826. Report by Thomas Shepard for the Executive Committee in Northampton, Massachusetts on April 3, 1826.

REPORT TO MESSRS. Thomas Shepherd, Elijah Bates, Augustus Collins and John Mills. 1827

H.R. – No. 53. Commonwealth of Massachusetts. 1827

AN ACT, To incorporate the Hampshire and Hampden Canal Company. 1827

H.R. – No. 67. Commonwealth of Massachusetts. 1827

RIVERS AND CANALS. Some remarks. Selected letters of Governor Clinton and Col. Baldwin. February, 1828.

Hillhouse, Hon. James. EXTENSION OF THE HAMPSHIRE AND HAMPDEN CANAL. 1827

H.R. – No. 413. CONNECTICUT RIVER LOCKS. Commonwealth of Massachusetts. 1828

CANAL NAVIGABLE. *Daily Hampshire Gazette*, 1786 – Present.

A list of canal related articles from the *Daily Hampshire Gazette.* 1835

A newspaper article from the *Daily Hampshire Gazette.* July 15, 1935

NORTHAMPTON – NEW HAVEN CANAL, *Daily Hampshire Gazette.*

Canal Navigable. First boat arrives in Northampton from Westfield on July 4th about 4 o'clock pulled by four gray houses and accompanied by sounds of bells, music and cannon. July 8, 1835.

WHEN NORTHAMPTON WAS A SEAPORT by Frank MacCarthy. The Springfield Union. This is a typed copy of *The Springfield Union* newspaper. Sunday, February 5, 1922

SOME ENGINEERING FEATURES OF THE OLD NORTHAMPTON CANAL by Charles Rufus Harte. Presented to the Forty-ninth Annual Meeting of the Connecticut Society of Civil Engineers. 1933.

This is a significant writing about the Northampton Canal by Charles Rufus Harte, member of the Connecticut Society of Civil Engineers; Engineer, The Connecticut Company, New Haven, Connecticut. Account includes survey, costs, reports, canal design, water supply, structures, the canal commission and specifications.

CONNECTICUT'S CANALS by Charles Rufus Harte. Reprinted from the Fifty-Fourth Annual Report of the Connecticut Society of Civil Engineers. Facts and figures not specifically referenced are from either the "Minutes" of the canal companies or from the "Account of the Farmington Canal". 1839.

THE OLD CANAL by Josephine E. Root. A short hand typed summary of the old canal, an ancient waterway, from New Haven, Conn. to Northampton, Mass. 1939.

WESTFIELD AND ITS HISTORICAL INFLUENCES. CHAPTER IV. WESTFIELD'S CANAL. 1922 pp 282 – 305. A history of the canal from the Connecticut River to Westfield and from New Haven Connecticut to Southwick in Massachusetts. Account includes stories about the 'First Cruise from the Port Of Westfield' in December 9, 1829. Rev. John H. Lockwood, D.D., Westfield and its Historic Influences.

CONNECTICUT RIVER. CANAL DAYS, Men Circumvent White Water. Marguerite Allis. pp. 30 – 35, 102 – 107, 125 – 134, 146, 226 – 227. Good account of the history along the Connecticut River. Many references to the methods used to move boats up or around the Connecticut River starting in 1792. References include Turners Fall Canal, South Hadley Canal, Bellows Falls and the Swift River between Hartford and Springfield where oxcarts pulled goods along the Podunk Trail. 1939.

AN ECONOMIC ANALYSIS OF THE NEW HAVEN AND NORTHAMPTON CANAL. Hecker, Louis L. January 30, 1967. NOTE: With Bibliographies.

CANAL DAYS. *Southwoods, A Journal for Country Living.* by Thelma Montavani, February 2000, pp. 4 – 5. A brief story about the canal through the Southwick.

IMAGES OF AMERICA, EASTHAMPTON. Edward Dwyer. A history of Easthampton including photographs of the remains of the canal in the late 19th century. 2000

A CANAL RUNS THROUGH IT. *The Valley Advocate News,* Tracing an old path . . . Canal boat design in folder. January 24, 2008.

THE NORTH CANAL LINE. The New York, New Haven and Hartford Line.

CANALS DAYS IN AMERICA. Harry Sinclair Drago. pp. 21 – 24. Stories about the history and romance of Old Towpaths and Waterways including a short history of the canal system between Long Island Sound, at New Haven, to Canada. 1972.

CANALS FOR A NATION, The Canal Era in the United States 1790 – 1860. Ronald E. Shaw. pp. 52 – 55. A brief history about the Farmington Canal Company and the Hampshire and Hampden Canal Company. 1990.

NEW HAVEN TO NORTHAMPTON. Josephine E. Root. A short paper about the canal given before the Easthampton Grange. 1939.

CANALS – MAPS

MAP OF THE FARMINGTON CANAL. Hummel, Ruth Sharp and Walter, Carl E. A serious and complete topographical canal map showing the route of the canal along with significant explanations of locks, brooks, wastes and the history of the system. 2000.

MAP OF THE HAMPSHIRE & HAMPDEN CANAL. Walter, Carl E. A serious and complete topographical canal map showing the route of the canal along with significant explanations of locks, brooks, weirs and the history of the system. 2006.

CANALS – INTERNET

HAMPSHIRE AND HAMPDEN CANALS, His Observations relative to the. 1828. De Witt Clinton Memoirs. http://www.history.rochester.edu/canal/bib/hosack/APPOL.htm. Governor Clinton's observations relative to the proposed Hampshire and Hampden Canals.

THE FARMINGTON CANAL. Connecticut Kelseys' Guide. http://www.kelseypub.com/ct-guide/historic/farmcanl.shtml. A brief story about the canal system with 2 half-plate pictures.

CANAL HISTORY REVISTED. Lock 12. http://acorn-online.com/100canal.htm. A picture and history of the canal remains preserved at Lock 12 Historical Park.

STUDENTS LEARN ABOUT THE 'DITCH BESIDE UHS'. YALE DAILY NEWS. April 20, 1998. Mackenzie Baris. http://yale.edu/ydn/paper/4.20.98/I-rditch.html. An article about a canal walk or 'ditch' across the street from the University Health Services building.

THE FARMINGTON CANAL 1822-1847: An Attempt At Internal Improvement. 1981. Yale-New Haven Teachers Institute. George M. Guignino. http://pclt.cis.yale.edu/ynhti/curriculum/units/1981/cthistory/81.ch.04.x.html. A scholarly narrative about the need for internal transportation in the 1800's.

CANAL EXHIBIT FOCUSES ON WORKING CONDITIONS. Nicole Licata. 1995. *The Yale Daily News.* http://www.hyale.edu/ydn/paper/4.3/4.3.95storyno.CB.html A local preservation group wants to renovate the canal. Yale is undecided.

FARMINGTON CANAL LOCK. January 16, 1973. Connecticut Historical Commission. Herbert C. Darbee. http://archnet.uconn.edu/topical/crm/conn/chc/farmcanl/. Period of significance: 1849 – 1877 with two pictures of the Cheshire Lock.

FARMINGTON CANAL BENEFITS ALL OF YALE. *The Yale Daily News*. November 1, 1996. Liz Alter. Rails-to-Trails article and the Farmington Canal Committee to build a trail useful to bikers and runners.

CANAL EXHIBIT FOCUSES ON WORKING CONDITIONS. April 3, 1995. *The Yale Daily News.* Nichole Licata. http://www.yale.edu/ydn/paper /4.3.95storyno.CB.Html. References an article in the Connecticut History Journal by Daniel Bendor '95 about Irish Labors on the canal.

MANHAN/NEW HAVEN & NORTHAMPTON CANAL RAIL TRAIL LETTERBOX. 2003 "Letterboxing North America" combines navigation with rubber stamp artistry for treasure hunting. The website has a rail trail map of the Manhan Rail Trail. http://bikeitorhikeit.org/manhan_new_haven_northampton_canal_rail_trail.htm .

RAILROADS - BOOKS

Armstrong, John H. The Railroad-What It Is, What It Does, (Bristol, CT: Simmons-EBoardman, 1978.)

Baker, George. The Formation of the New England Railroad Systems, (Cambridge, MA: Harvard University Press. 1937.)

Beauregard, Mark W., Railroad Stations of New England Today, (Flanders, NJ. Railroad Avenue Enterprises. Inc. 1979.)

Harlow, Alvin F., Steelways of New England, (New York: Creative Age, 1946.)

Holbrook, Stewart H., The Story of American Railroads, (New York: Bonanza Books. 1947.)

Hubbard, Freeman. Encyclopedia of North American Railroading, (New York: McGraw-Hill, 1981.)

Jenson, Oliver. The American Heritage History of Railroads, (New York: American Heritage, 1975.)

Karr, Ronald Dale. Lost Railroads of New England, (Pepperell, MA: Branch Line Press. 1989.)

Nelligan, Tom. The Valley Railroad Story, (New York: Quadrant Press, 1983.)

Nock, Oswald S., Railways of the USA, (New York: Hastings House, 1979.)

Ogburn, Charlton. Railroads: The Great American Adventure, (Washington, D.C.: National Geographic Society, 1937.)

Turner, M. Gregg and Jacobus, Melancthon, Connecticut Railroads An Illustrated History, (Manchester, CT: Allied Printing Services. A publication by The Connecticut Historical Society, 1989.)

Pavlucik, Andrew J., The New Haven Railroad, A Fond Look Back, (New Haven: Pershing Press, 1978.)

Roy, John H, Jr., A Field Guide to Southern New England Railroad Depots and Freight Houses, (Pepperell, MA: Branch Line Press. 2007.)

Weller, John L., The New Haven Railroad, Its Rise and Fall, New York: Hastings House, 1969.)

Withington, Sidney. The First Twenty Years of Railroads in Connecticut, (Tercentenary Commission, State of Connecticut, New Haven: Yale University Press, 1935.)

BIKE AND RAIL TRAILS - INTERNET

- **CONNECTICUT BICYCLE COALITION.**

- **DEP PURCHASE A 9.5 MILE ADDITION TO THE FARMINGTON CANAL TRAIL.** December 4, 1998. dep.state.ct.us/whatshap/press/1998/as120498.htm. A narrative about the opening of the Farmington Canal Trail and Greenway located on the abandoned Boston and Maine (B&M) rail line in Cheshire and Southington.

- **FARMINGTON CANAL HERITAGE TRAIL.** www.dmvct.org/kids/trail/farmington%20heritage1.htm. An abandoned railbed converted to multi-use greenway in Simsbury.

- **THE INTERNATIONAL MOUNTAIN BIKE ASSOCIATION.**

- **THE LEAGUE OF MOUNTAIN BIKE ASSOCIATION.**

- **MASS BIKE.**

- **NEW ENGLAND MOUNTAIN BIKE ASSOCIATION.**

- **NORTHAMPTON CYCLING CLUB.**

• **THE NORTHERN CANAL LINE. NHRHTA PUBLICATION.** www.nhrhta.org/htdocs/map.htm. A map of the New Haven Railroad/NHRHTA Publications by Line.

• **OPEN STREET MAP.** www.openstreetmap.org. A user friendly map whereby individuals can interact by being able to update or add significant features. Map shows East Coast Greenway and other bike trails.

• **RAILS-TO-TRAILS CONSERVANCY.**

• **SOUTHERN CONNECTICUT CYCLE CLUB.**

• **SUFFIELD BIKE & RECREATION TRAIL HISTORY.** Town of Suffield. http://www.suffieldtownhall.com/suffieldbiketrail.htm. Suffield Trail to be connected to the Farmington Valley Greenway trail ultimately to Southwick. Massachusetts.

HISTORICAL SOCIETIES ALONG THE CANAL

• **NEW HAVEN.** New Haven Museum & Historical Society, 114 Whitney Ave., New Haven CT. 203 562-4183. www.newhavenmuseum.org

• **HAMDEN.** Miller Memorial Central Library, 2901 Dixwell Ave, Hamden, CT. 06518. 203-287-2680. http://newhavenmuseum.org/ www.hamdenlibrary.org/historicalsociety.

• **CHESHIRE.** The Cheshire Historical Society, 43 Church Dr., Cheshire, CT 06410. 203-272-2574. http://www.cheshirehistory.org/

• **SOUTHINGTON.** The Southington Historical Society, 239 Main St., Southington, CT 06489. 860-621-4811. http://southingtonhistory.org/

• **PLAINVILLE.** Plainville Historical Center, 29 Pierce St., Plainville, CT 06062. 860-747-6577. http://www.plainvillehistory.org/

• **FARMINGTON.** Farmington Historical Society, 138 Main St., Farmington, CT 860-678-1645. http://farmingtonhistoricalsociety-ct.org/

• **AVON.** The Avon Historical Society, P.O. Box 448, Avon, CT 06001. 860 678-7621. www.avonhistoricalsociety.org.

• **SIMSBURY.** Simsbury Historical Society, 800 Hopmeadow St., Simsbury, CT 06070. 860-658-2500. http://simsburyhistory.org/

• **EAST GRANBY.** East Granby Historical Society, 24 Center St., East Granby, CT 06026. 860-653-3002. http://www.eastgranby.com/historicalsociety/.

• **GRANBY.** Salmon Brook Historical Society, 208 Salmon Brook St., Granby, CT. 860 653-9713. www.salmonbrookhistorical.org.

• **SUFFIELD.** Suffield Historical Society, 232 Main St., P.O. Box 893, Suffield, CT 06078. 860-668-5256. http://www.suffieldhistoricalsociety.org/

• **SOUTHWICK.** Southwick Historical Society, Inc., 86 College Hwy., P.O. Box 323, Southwick, MA 01077. 413-569-0436. http://www.southwickhistoricalsociety.org/ .

• **WESTFIELD.** Western Hampden Historical Society, 87 South Maple St., Westfield, MA 01085 413-562-0612. http://www.thedeweyhouse.org/

• **SOUTHAMPTON.** Southampton Historical Society, 210 College Hwy., Southampton, MA 01073. http://www.town.southampton.ma.us/dbcc/historical.php

• **EASTHAMPTON.** Easthampton Historical Society, 7 Holyoke St., Easthampton, MA 01027. 413-527-3108. http://www.museumsusa.org/museums/info/1160973

• **NORTHAMPTON.** Forbes Library, 20 West St., Northampton, MA 01060. 413-527-3108. Historic Northampton website: www.historic-northampton.org/.

RAIL - TRAIL LINKS

http://www.a1trails.com/rail/

http://www.americantrails.org/

http://www.bikeitorhikeit.org/

http://www,columbiagreenway.org/

http://www.connecticutriver.us/l

http://www.ct.gov/deep/cwp/

http://www.ctbikeroutes.org/

http://www.cyclopaedia.fr/

http://www.eastgranby.com/

http://www.farmingtoncanal.org/

http://www.fntg.net/

http://www.greenway.org/

http://www.hamdentrails.com/

http://www.manhanrailtrail.org/

http://www.mapmyride.com/us/

http://www.massbike.org/

http://www.masscentralrailtrail.org/

http://www.newenglandbicycle.com/

http://www.pedalparadise.wordpress.com/

http://www.plainvillegreenway.blogspot.com/

http://www.railstotrails.org/

http://www.southington.org/LinearTrail

http://www.southwickrailtrail.org/

http://www.traillink.com/

http://www.trails.com/

http://www.visitconnecticut.com/state/biking/

http://www.wordpress.shorelinegreenwaytrail.org/

RAILROAD LINKS

http://www.abandonedrails.com/Connecticut

http://www.akrailroad.com/

http://www.amtrak.com/

http://www.ctrailroads.com/

http://www.images.lib.uconn.edu/

http://www.masscentralrailtrail.org

http://www.mta.info/

http://www.newbritainstation.com/

http://www.nhrhta.org/

http://www.nhrhta.org/

http://www.northernrailservices.com/

http://www.pinsly.com/companies/pvrr/

http://www.pvls.org/

http://www.railfanguides.us/

http://www.railpictures.net/

http://www.railroad.net/

http://www.railroads.uconn.edu/

http://www.southington.org/TrainDepot

http://www.trainweb.org/crocon/CanalLine/

ABOUT THE AUTHOR

Bob Madison is not only a hiker and bicyclist; he is an avid sailor and skier. The genesis for this rail-to-trail book starts back when he was in High School. Daily he would unknowingly walk across the old canal before catching a bus to school. Later in life, after college and a family, he rediscovered the canal and also discovered that it slowly was neglected or destroyed by developers. Bob's bicycling experience is centered west of the Connecticut River. He has been researching the canal's route along the trails and byways of the New Haven & Northampton Canal System. He has biked, hiked, bushwhacked and driven back and forth along all 86 miles of the canal and the old railroad system. In addition, as a hiker and Scoutmaster, he has hiked trails in Philmont, New Mexico, the Presidential Range of the White Mountains in New Hampshire, New England sections of the Appalachian Trail and along the Metacomet Trail. As an avid sailor, Bob was a Yacht Club Commodore; Commander at a local U.S. Coast Guard Auxiliary Flotilla and he also teaches boat safety at area colleges. As a watercolorist he is an active member of Agawam Community Artists. Bob has degrees from the University of Hartford, American International College and Western New England University. He is retired from both Pratt & Whitney [Aircraft] division of United Technologies and the Commonwealth of Massachusetts, Public Employee Retirement Administration Commission. Bob is a member of the Columbia Greenway Rail Trail and he hopes you will enjoy your hike and bicycle ride through history from the shores of New Haven's harbor to the banks of the Connecticut River in Northampton.

Marine watercolors of modern sailboats on Long Island Sound by the author.

NOTES